MULTIDIMENSIONAL LENS

PRACTICAL IDEAS FOR SPIRITUAL CO-CREATION

DAVID COLLURA

Mosaic
WELLNESS AND EDUCATION

Cover design by Carol Rambaldi.

ISBN 978-1-972698-00-6

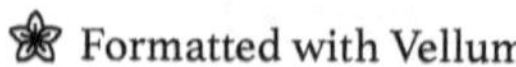 Formatted with Vellum

For Ash

CONTENTS

INTRODUCTION

If you tell me this is a bad work, I won't contradict you. I have problems with it. But somehow, it agrees with me. This is a book about taking the risk of trusting your experiences.

It is a heady and electric sensation to trust your life and where it has taken you. To look backward and inward, breathe it in, and let it back into the world without manicure. This book is a journey much as life has been a journey.

This book is, first, a personal work. I measure its value in honesty and philosophical self-searching. It is my attempt to share what I feel to be the best parts of myself. It is my hope that it creates space in a world that can feel increasingly crowded.

This is also a snapshot of my spiritual and interior life. Rugged and imperfect with weird edges that don't always line up. But like an organism that has seen itself, it strives to redouble its vitality and make more of this life. It seeks to honor glimpses it has found, to share back treasures that are available to all of us when we make incremental adjustments to our understanding; playing with and rearticulating our lives, ourselves, and our relationships.

Last, it is an offering. I bring the bizarre bounty and place it in your hands. There is that moment where our fingers touch and the exchange is made. I don't really know what it is I am giving you, but it is something true and honest and of myself. Take with it what you will.

Like this book, my background is something I have struggled to accept for many years. I have given classes on topics related to spirituality, energy and non-ordinary states of awareness for more than fifteen years, previously with the International Academy of Consciousness and more recently with Mosaic Wellness and Education, which I founded in 2018 with my wife Ashley and three of our colleagues. It is a major part of my life that I have been reticent to share with others, or even let them know about.

As I have grown myself and my spiritual life, I have been able to broach this topic a bit more with friends and colleagues, letting the hemispheres of my life breathe just a bit. At the same time, I have found my practice become more squishy, more interesting, and more compatible with other ways of seeing things. In the last several years, I have focused more critically on the core ideas and practices which will translate into meaningful outcomes for one's personal life and for our communities and societies at large.

Hopefully, the ideas, stories, and sentiments of this book will connect with anyone who is open to hearing the personal ideas of another, knowing that they will color outside the lines and go to some weird places. At the same time, these ideas will naturally find a foothold with people who are spiritually open, curious, or adventurous.

These are my personal ideas; in a spirit of authenticity, I have tried not to be too didactic or hierarchical in how I present them. They are ultimately a tissue graft of my intellectual and emotional life. According to your needs as a reader, you can think of these ideas as a loose open-source framework for engaging life in many dimensions; or as a living memoir of a fellow traveler; or as a dialogue between the two.

However you see me, I hope to see you, and I hope that you find room to breathe in these pages.

1

CO-CREATION

So let it be clumsy. I am misshapen like a dirty potato. I want all the dirty potatoes to show up. We'll show up before rural headlights like zombies. But then, believe it or not, we will sing our hearts out in a queer harmony. In a key that mankind has never heard before.

THERE IS SO MUCH that we want. And so much that the world seems to offer in dwindling supply. We want to explore and see breathtaking vistas. We want to make great discoveries that expand our understanding of the world. And we want to transcend, as a society, to something that makes more sense. Something less acrimonious and wasteful. Something we would be glad to be a part of.

And yet, as humanity works its way across the planet, things have become dulled. Our landscapes have been mapped, by man and machine and satellite. Our discoveries are fewer and more incremental. Our rational culture somehow leaves us feeling desiccated, reduced to resources in a capital machine.

Our modern world is a paved world - asphalt, commerce, and a zero sum game.

It may not always feel this way. We enjoy our days, each with their unique character. And we look back on history and feel grateful for all the practical improvements we have come to enjoy. But we are also concerned about the world; and we feel our purpose is entwined with how we can change the world.

While we do not feel this way all the time, this is still an enduring sentiment in our world today. We need solutions which are individual and collective, solutions which can bridge the many divides that speckle our human brotherhood. As the liberal pockets of society grow increasingly secular and the conservative pockets remain steadfast in their traditions, it seems more than ever that we need a concerted effort to bridge divides and open up possibilities for healthy new developments as a collective humanity.

Harmonizing our fractured world is a huge project with many scenarios. Yet, perhaps counterintuitively, we will need to start with small, personal changes of mindset. We need to align ourselves on some common principles of thought which will help us to generate a more meaningful stream of dialogue and individual expression. If not, we may get stuck rehashing or arguing about external events and how best to interpret them. Let's move beyond that, and we may find ourselves co-creating new possibilities and, just maybe, a warmer and more healthy world.

I am going to introduce three small mindset shifts that can produce a big difference. They will form the basis for how the rest of this work will proceed.

Mindset Shifts

The first mindset shift lets go of the idea that any human being or human life is more important than any other. This idea often suggests that we lower our personal status and realize that distant others are as important as we are; but in this case, I want to explore the converse. Our lives are as valid and fundamental as the lives of anyone else, in any part of the world. Nobody is above us. No life is more important than ours.

This may be considered "main character energy" or a narcissistic outlook, but it can be adopted in a healthy and truly useful way. When this idea is considered in a mature, balanced way, we may see that we were giving too much of our personal power to those in positions of authority, prestige, or influence. We may feel more of our energy enter into our lives. We will begin to see the value of investing in our lives, in this very life, here and now. This is the first mindset shift for co-creation. I call it the **primary self**.

I ADVISE a second mindset shift where we untether ourselves from the dominance of **reference knowledge** - that is, become less personally, emotionally reliant on any fixed, external body of ideas. At the end of the day, we are our own craftspeople of thought and understanding. While we may emulate the ideas of others, or use them as inspiration for our own thought creations, we will always be unique at our essence, and unique in how we produce and act upon our thoughts. For this reason, we will benefit when we shift our thinking away from central dogmas of thought - be they scientific, philosophical, political, religious or otherwise - and value more our own **personal ideas**. Personal ideas are exactly this: the ideas and insights that we have created ourselves. They are truly ours and belong to us. Rather than defaulting to ideas that we feel are legitimized by outside organizations, we can reaffirm the value of our own ideas. We are creative people, we are intelligent people, we are innovating people, and when we affirm the value of our mind's creations, we activate our vibrant souls.

I want you to develop and value your personal ideas because you are important and intelligent and I feel your creative capacity is essential. If you are engaged with your creative capacities, you will be engaged in life, and you will be a contributor of culture, of new ideas, of revitalized relationships. You will produce that lifeblood that this world needs to stay healthy and alive.

I want to differentiate personal ideas from mere opinions. As you read this, maybe you are thinking of people who present forceful ideas in a way that seems unconstructive. Rather than creating culture, they alienate people by imposing their ideas on others. Their ideas don't build relationships, but just reverberate across those who do or don't agree. What is missing from the ideas of these people?

A forceful opinion is not the same thing as a personal idea. I would say that a **personal idea** has two facets: first, it is your own idea that is authentic to you. And second, a personal idea is one that is steeped in self-awareness of your own personal history. It is expressed through a medium of authenticity and usually entails some personal vulnerability. If we remove our personal history and unique story from our ideas, we cut out a huge part of what makes those ideas meaningful and vital. Our lived experiences are the vital background of our ideas. When we divorce our ideas from our rich and complicated person-hood, our thoughts become disconnected from our world and are more likely to have violent qualities.

Conversely, when we are open about our life experiences and background when we share our ideas, we avoid the pitfall of giving a boring philosophy lecture. We make the discussion fun and fascinating: a window into another person's world, rich and alive and current. And we will more likely share these ideas freely, without the pressure for others to adopt them, so avoiding any violence, coercion, or degradation of others. In this way, we create a pattern where people can share their ideas, create new ideas, and hear what others have to say, in a manner that is interesting and fun and engaging. The key to personal ideas is to be vulnerable, open and self-aware - expressing something true to our primary self.

In this way, we are not just sharing our ideas but in fact we are sharing the **vital energy** of ourselves. When people share of themselves, vitally, it is an act of creation. It is often beautiful; it can become a cosmic or mesmerizing experience. It gives both parties more energy. It is life-affirming and hopeful. And it is absolutely fundamental as a human experience of life.

THE THIRD MINDSET shift is to value our **local experience**. We should view our personal, lived reality as being as valid, as important, as instrumental as any other events taking place in our world.

This may be highly counterintuitive. When we look out into the world around us, we see many other scenarios in the world: those with greater influence, more political power or leverage, and, of course, those with untold wealth and its material comforts (and self-determination of lifestyle). We look out into the world and see others with more - and we see ourselves with less.

However, this is a flawed way to look at things. I was speaking with a friend once who works for a luxury goods company, and he was remarking on the status of the wealthy in this world. He said something like, "this is their world. We are living in their world, and they have all the power." While I understood this on an economic level, I reject the idea that our lived experience of reality is in any way inferior to that of any other person who has more money, power, or any other perceived attribute. The truth is, **all local experience is valid and fundamental.**

Just like before, where we see ourselves as the true main

character in our own life - when we value and recognize our primary self - our personal experience, here in this moment, becomes every bit as essential, fundamental, and meaningful as any other. This moment does not need to exist as a subservient to any other moment in our life. One idea that is a helpful artic-ulation of this concept is Arthur Koestler's idea of 'holonic' reality (which I encountered through the work of Ken Wilber). He says that reality is composed of wholes ('holons') which are themselves pieces of other wholes. So, while this moment is one part of this hour, and this hour is part of this day, and this day is part of this year - each element is completely whole and fundamental in its own right.

So, I am advocating for a mindset shift where we recognize ourselves as primary in our lives; validate and affirm our personal ideas; and validate our local experience as funda-mental and truly meaningful.

Why does this matter? Why am I taking the time to talk about this? Because without these ideas, we may continually look to outside references or events for guidance as the basis for our lives. Instead, we will develop a more co-creative culture and outlook when we see this moment as completely whole; when we see this experience with these people as absolutely fundamental; and when we see our personal ideas, which we reflect in that moment, to be entirely valid reflections of our most authentic understanding of existence at that moment in time.

Through these notions of embracing the **primary self, personal ideas** and **local experience,** we can de-condition ourselves from hierarchies and limitations imposed from outside of us and which prevent us from truly embracing our authentic lived moments and the individual insights we derive from them.

Spirituality

The three mindset shifts from the previous section touch on important personal topics. Where should I focus my energy? Which ideas are true, or which ideas should I emphasize as I live my life? What is important? What is my relationship with the many facets of my own life? These sorts of questions connect with us on an intimate level and concern who we are and how we live our lives. In many ways, they concern our sense of spirituality.

There are many ways of defining spirituality. Here is how I think about it: Spirituality is your intimate relationship with your life, your world, yourself, and other people. It has a softer, more nuanced and personal connotation than religion, which tends to emphasize particular beliefs, customs, or group affiliations. While everybody has their own distinct religious or spiritual orientation, I think it is important to wade into these waters if we want to co-create new possibilities for ourselves and others. If we aren't willing to bring our spiritualities into the dialogue, things may stay too superficial. In some ways, I feel we don't really see who a person is, we don't really build trust, until we touch on that personal space that we reserve for spirituality.

Spirituality is a space where we can easily overcome the boundaries of our paved world. Remember that the paved world represents a desiccation of our opportunities to explore, discover, create meaning, and generate harmonious culture. In many respects, these goals are at one with our spiritual pursuits. We fundamentally wish to explore because it is a spiritual calling. We wish for discoveries because they provide a sense of transcendence. A sense of meaning is essential to who we are and how we are living our lives. And a harmonious culture requires a set of core ideas that speak to us on a deep, abiding level.

One of the biggest challenges of spirituality is that it has become deeply politicized throughout the course of human history. Our religions are filled with pressures to conform, to align, to indoctrinate to a single system. I am not criticizing religion outright, and if a particular tradition works well for you, I offer you every encouragement to continue as long as it serves you. However, in my experience, spirituality is at its core a personal and fluid journey. We are fluid creatures - our visions and ideas change over time. More shallow things change over the days, deeper things change like tectonics over the decades. Some things remain persistent, deep within us, our whole lives. Spirituality is like this - we are dynamic landscapes, and our spiritualities should be a reflection of our personal ideas. We are creative beings, so - let us be creative and spiritual together.

My Personal Ideas

So, we are spiritual beings and I have shared some mindset shifts to help catalyze co-creation among people. The challenge now is that we are not all speaking the same language. How do we co-create when our spiritualities are distinct from one another? We have differing worldviews and we attribute different causations to the universe.

The challenging answer is that *we don't have to be the same.* We can learn to share and co-create while being in different places, spiritually. What we need to do is *evolve* our way of communicating and relating to one another so that we are no longer stymied by the natural diversity of viewpoint that comes from our personal creative journeys.

Where do we go from here? How do we reconcile our seemingly intractable differences and find a common ground to build from? It might seem we need some focal structure to facilitate it: a tree to build ourselves around. But really, we need to develop a forest of trees. We each need to provide our personal ideas amply into a shared space so that we can all get to know each other and co-create collectively.

To this end, in the spirit of co-creation and personal ideas and local experience, I offer this current work. These are my personal ideas, and the ones I find most critical, meaningful, truly insightful for myself. I hope that they offer some possibilities for you. I fully acknowledge that the ideas I provide from this point forward may be challenging, heretical, or preposterous to a number of readers. I continue to submit myself as a story to share. As an individual to be listened to. As a viewpoint to be known. If you feel these ideas are of use to you, by all means draw these ideas into your personal workspace and start building your own experiences around them. Play with them to create your own innovations and personal ideas. But most of all, don't feel pressured to align with anything I have to say from this point forward.

Multidimensional Lens

Before diving headlong into my personal ideas, I want to share a bit of my backstory and provide a loose framework for the universe in which my forthcoming ideas will exist.

As a young man, I graduated from college with a burning desire to understand what my life was about and what really mattered to me. I was, basically, asking myself those very questions I posed earlier this chapter as spiritual in nature. I explored many different traditions, philosophies, and experiences. Eventually, I found my way to an organization that taught about energy and out-of-body experience, among other topics. This organization had significant cultural limitations; but there was no denying that my experiences and developments through that organization were facilitating some kind of essential growth and progress for me as a person. **Cooking with gas**, I have come to call this concept. The notion was that there are many ideas, practices, and traditions - but for my personal needs, they always felt too theoretical, too limited, too ineffectual. But what really impacted me was 'cooking with gas' - applying ideas and practices which impacted my life in a material way. Factors that genuinely expressed a transformative potential. That made me feel different, think differently, express a renewed and more authentic layer of myself. The practices I encountered at this organization, and which I have adapted and re-expressed in the body of this text, made this effect on me. Notably, I did not apply this term conceptually but retrospectively: *the work changed me; I felt these changes; my life growing lithe and clear-headed; the right phrase seemed to be 'cooking with gas'*.

Based on my experiences 'cooking with gas' for the last 15+ years, I have boiled down the essential concepts, experiences, and practices of this viewpoint for engaging with reality. I call it the **Multidimensional Lens**. This represents a small number of fixed concepts which define the core boundaries of how I understand reality to operate in a manner beyond this purely physical realm.

The Multidimensional Lens is composed of the following three principles:

1. Energy - we have a personal energetic system and we are living in a world with underlying energetic ecosystems at play. We will explore the ramifications of this principle in great detail, and illustrate several powerful applications to life.

2. Persistence of Life - we existed before our physical birth; we will exist following our physical death.
   This life is just one in a collection of lifetimes that

we are living out in our evolutionary curriculum as multidimensional people.

3. Multidimensional Support - in addition to this population of physical people, there are nonphysical populations who are not currently undergoing physical lifetimes. Among these nonphysical people are balanced, healthy communities who are already existing as harmonious societies in this nonphysical, energetic context. These individuals are actively involved in the facilitation of our multidimensional growth and evolutionary coursework here in the physical world. They are commonly referred to as "spirit guides" or "spirit helpers".

This is me putting my cards on the table. That's about as weird as it gets. I am going to unpack these ideas throughout the book. But I do not want you thinking I have a typical or mainstream outlook before I blindside you with some unconventional ideas.

When I share these ideas with people, they often respond with things like, "well, maybe it's not exactly that," or "maybe you're interpreting it this way, but it's actually simpler than that." And I encourage everyone to develop their personal ideas as they encounter my own expression. But this is not new or flighty for me. I've had an enduring relationship with these ideas for more than a decade. It is my understanding that I have meaningful relationships which extend beyond this physical context. I know that sounds weird, but these are enduring facets of my reality, co-developed over many years of personal lived experiences, and I don't see myself discarding them because someone objects the first time they hear them.

So, the multidimensional lens contains three core concepts. The first is energy, which is probably easiest to swallow - it is a believable possibility. It is simply a question of 'layering' an additional system of functioning onto the human being (or living entity, if we wish to indicate plants and animals). We have a circulatory system, a skeletal system, an endocrine system, and so on... and a system of energy, as well. Anybody who is open to the principles of yoga, tai chi, or acupuncture would theoretically consider this, as these practices are based on the concept of a human energy system.

The next two concepts may be harder for some to entertain. Do not worry - there is no expectation that you agree with these or take them at face value. I don't expect you to *ever* adopt this lens if it does not benefit you. However, this is a way to create safety because I am creating a transparent paradigm with the clear indication that nobody is expecting you to adopt any or all of it. You are, however, welcome to utilize these concepts in all or in part (perhaps being open to energy, while believing that the other two concepts are simply too strange to stomach) and continue enjoying the content of this book as, among other things, an anthropological curiosity and a chance to better know a fellow human being.

Intermediary Metaphysics

I do feel that concepts 2 and 3 of the Multidimensional Lens are quite important. As you will see throughout this book, they are essential to many of the personal ideas I will present which are powerfully useful for understanding and living life more effectively. Moreover, I want to point out that these ideas - regarding multiple-life cycles and the reality of communities which exist beyond the physical dimension - occupy an important place in a spiritual worldview which is often overlooked. I call it 'intermediary metaphysics'.

Many people are open to the idea of energy or the notion that our intentions can directly affect an outcome, such as a random number generator. I call this 'adjacent metaphysics' - it refers to the idea that there are nonphysical realities and phenomena which exist very close to our physical systems and can have some limited impression on the physical world around us. Conversely, people are comfortable musing about the great origin of all things - the unmoved mover, the first gasp of consciousness, or an absolute and ultimate understanding of life. I call this 'distant metaphysics' - they deal with concepts which exist beyond the physical and extend to the most far-flung reaches. People are more comfortable with these two polar edges of metaphysics, but they often become squeamish talking about how the sausage is made in all the spiritual space between - what we do in the time between lifetimes, or what individuals are like who are not currently living out a physical lifetime. To this discomfort, I ask rhetorically, "who's afraid of intermediary metaphysics?" By deepening our understanding of multidimensionality, of energy, of intermediary metaphysics, I feel that we can mature, clarify, and amplify our understanding of reality in a broader sense.

And yet, embedded in our people, these ideas may not be so exotic or novel as many of us may think. An interesting statistic is that one third of adults in the United States believe in reincarnation according to a Pew Research poll in 2021, so these ideas may be more commonplace than we would initially assume. But people typically do not share their spiritual framework openly, which makes it harder to understand how everyone understands the spiritual realities at play in our world and beyond.

While the multidimensional lens is a sort of 'spiritual philosophy', note that it can be aligned with various spiritual or religious traditions which may already connect on certain concepts to some degree. This will allow us to already interface with one another as spiritual people with the understanding that we can utilize a common language between us.

Regardless of your spiritual worldview, I warmly invite you to continue with this text. I have put amplitudes of myself into it. This is my personal work, and I am sharing myself freely. You are welcomed to sit and enjoy the warmth of human company. I believe there is a natural edification when we come to know one another as fellows in this human endeavor.

2

NONVIOLENCE

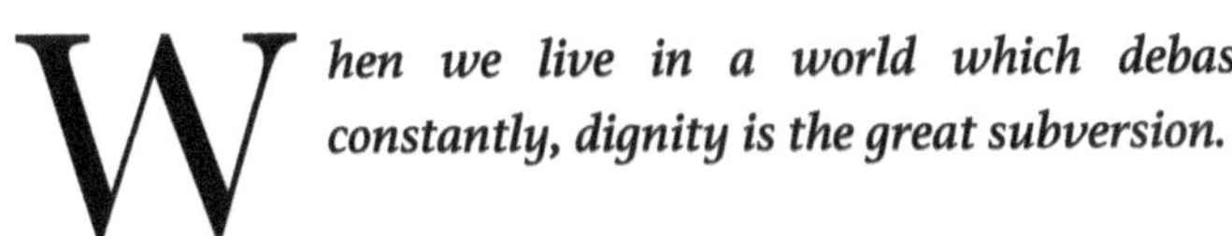

THROUGHOUT THIS BOOK, I will be sharing my personal ideas related to a body of spiritual concepts and realities as I recognize them. Following on the ideas of the previous chapter - primary self, personal ideas, and local experience - it is not my hope that you simply adopt the ideas in this book and wear them as your own. Rather, I wish to share my viewpoints freely so that people can experience my personal reality secondhand, perhaps access new perspectives on their own reality, and arrive at novel insights and co-create some new possibilities for themselves and others.

Nevertheless, I want to use this chapter to explore several core ideas which are, for me, essential to how we should negotiate the sharing and exchange of spiritual ideas. For this purpose - and many others, as well - I believe a set of core principles related to nonviolence will be essential to creating a healthy, civil, mature space where individuals are able to freely explore their own and others' ideas without fear of punishment or ostracism. Violence can operate in a variety of forms - all of which are some kind of attack on the dignity of our personhood - and so it is in fact a deeply interesting and meaningful discourse to unpack nonviolence as it pertains to the concerns of this text.

Nonviolence feels, to me, like an ancient technology of immense power and potential. People talk about which technology is going to revolutionize the next century. I feel that, if we are able to truly stick the landing and apply it in a mature and evolving fashion, nonviolence will truly be the revolutionary technology that will reshape our world. Nonviolence will be the greatest technological breakthrough of the third millennium.

You Do Not Need to Change

First, I want to tell you that you do not need to change. You do not need to do anything different. You do not need to be anything different. You are whole and complete and valid, right now. I don't care if you are wearing dirty clothes or if you can't think clearly or if you are in a bad mood. None of this means you have to change. You are completely valid, right now; now and forever.

I want to say this outright and emphasize it because this text concerns itself with some spiritual ideas. And where there is spirituality, I feel we are always so close to prescriptions on how we should live. Who we should be. What ideals or virtues we should embody. These can be explicitly called out in the form of edicts or principles; or they can be tacit, underlying expectations embedded in how certain ideas are explained or presented. Regardless of how it happens, I believe this is a form of violence against people. It is a form of violence against you, and I want to clear the space of any lingering specter of coercion before continuing.

So, I will say it one more time: you are complete. You are whole. You are valid. You don't have to change. You don't have to change for me, and I am not asking you to change. One of the ideas that helps me bring this home is an insight I had during a course several years ago.

Circle of Free Will

I imagined a land that represents a person's internal world. And inside that world, there is one part of that person that represents their free will. Let's say it is a well. It is a well from which that person draws their original thoughts, ideas, and insights, and channels them to make their decisions. This process is sacred. It is not anyone's right to violate another's **sovereign free will.**

So, I imagined that there is a dotted line circled around that person's well - it represents the boundary of their free will. And the idea is that nobody is allowed to cross that line into the free will space of anyone else. Regardless of what we feel and what we want for that other person - we have to relinquish control when it comes to that other person's free will. If we needed to restrain them for safety's sake, for example, this would be a case of containing their behavior, but still would not represent an attempt to *coerce them* or *contaminate the integrity of their decision-making.* This model of sovereign free will and sanctity of personal choice is a helpful one for ensuring we maintain a healthy and liberated relationship free of brainwashing or other coercive behaviors. It also allows us to give up on misguided attempts to influence the choices of others when it is outside the realm of our nonviolence. We designate the space where we can ethically influence outcomes and help people to understand - and go no further.

We will discuss this idea in greater detail below and see that, when we incorporate the concept of energies, it becomes more alive and meaningful than we may have anticipated before.

Using this idea of the sacred well, the sovereignty of self, we can refine the idea of nonviolence into a more mature direction. Nonviolence is not about preventing conflict or disagreement. It does not seek stasis or fixity of life. Nonviolence is not a negation of the vibrant and dynamic experiences we pursue, and our right to express ourselves to others.

Rather, nonviolence is about having a more mature viewpoint regarding the nature of reality in the context of many constituent agents taking part. It is about understanding how our world is a network of intersecting journeys. Each of us has our own individual path where we intimately explore and express ourselves. Nonviolence is about affirming a *sanctity* of the paths that exist in this network. It is about deepening our appreciation for each person's free will and their essential dignity and their path of growth.

Condemning to Helping

On a related note, we can consider how we often make demands of others, or how we seek to regulate human behavior by saying it is "right" or "wrong" to act a certain way. Many people complain or condemn when someone upsets them or causes harm to others. While condemnation may come from a constructive intention, it can be seen as a way to impose one's will on the behavior of others, which has its own subtle connotation of violence. This often leaves both parties feeling alienated toward one another.

An alternative, which may be more effective and nonviolent in the long run, would be to shift our mindset from **controlling** others to **requesting** changes from others. We shift the focus away from the "wrongness" that the "perpetrator" is doing and instead focus on the human needs that are being harmed or unmet. I find this is a healthier and more effective way to approach disagreements or conflict. Rather than exposing a monstrous perpetrator, we expose a hurting human being, which is an image we are naturally wired to attend to and care for. It may be a challenge to communicate our needs in this way, but perhaps vulnerability is the price of admission for the possibility of true resolution and community.

This is a concept we see reflected in the tradition of nonviolent communication by Marshall Rosenberg as well as the practice of satyagraha created by Mahatma Gandhi. One of the great essences of nonviolence is to shift away from a modality of enforcing others; and to shift toward communicating to foster awareness and care toward others.

Nonviolence and Life After Death

Referring to our Multidimensional Lens, the second principle is that our life persists across time, beyond the reaches of physical birth and death. As a result of this, we can see that using violence against another person will never be the most efficient path forward. They will, and we will, go on and on, beyond this lifetime and into the next. When we utilize violence, condemnation, or coercion, we are typically ejecting people (and the meaning we have ascribed them) out of our psyche and out of some area of our lives. But they will never truly vanish, and we will find ourselves (and the world) reckoning with these people well into the future.

We are all victims of our own immaturities. And the only lasting path forward is to grow and mature. People grow best when they are in touch with their essential dignity and a spiritual wellbeing. If we attempt to override someone's free will or essential dignity, we are trying - and sometimes succeeding, unfortunately - to convince somebody that they are a lesser being, inferior to their true nature. These setbacks will always be temporary, however, as everyone will learn and mature in the fullness of time. A nonviolent perspective is capable of seeing everyone's intrinsic value and will work to amplify their essential dignity to create powerful, edifying relationships and act on the possibility of new collective outcomes.

By developing our internal condition of nonviolence and expressing ourselves toward others and toward our world in a nonviolent manner, we create a fecund space for authenticity, honesty, and healing, and clarity of thought that can enable real progress in our context of experience.

Willful Personal Change

At this point, I have told you directly that you don't need to change, and I have encouraged an intimate exploration of nonviolence which aims to prevent us from coercing others to behave or change in any way that violates their free will. At this point, you might even suspect that I don't want anyone to change - that I am in fact opposed to any sort of change. There are some who take this point of view, believing that we are essentially perfect deep down and the world is perfect in its imperfections.

In some ways, from a perspective of nonviolence, this is true, and reflects some of the ideas above. However, I find that my personal journey through life is woven with a thread of meaning that drives itself through a series of personal changes. That is, my life has become more meaningful as I have changed as a person. And as I have changed as a person, my life has become more meaningful. I have matured in ways that have allowed me to rise above my pain and frustration. I have been able to achieve greater consistency and a healthier level of self-determination, which has made my life much more satisfying;

when I was younger, I felt (and still feel, at times) like a ship lost at sea.

So I do care deeply for personal change. I care about the possibilities it provides to improve our common experience of life. I care about its ability to restore and redeem our past experiences, folding them beautifully into the present in our multidimensional spiritual landscape. I care about the sense of wholeness - not just during the occasional amplified spiritual experience, but as a consistent sentiment throughout my life - that change allows us to access.

However, I want this change to be yours. It will belong to you. It will come from you. It will be driven by your own insights, and leveraged through your own intimate free will. I will not tell you to change. I will share my ideas freely with care. Care for you and for your possibilities. But without the expectation that you will be of any less value, ever, regardless of your behavior or perceived performance.

By telling you that the change is yours to have, I hope to create a space where you can connect to yourself authentically and develop your own personal journey through your evolutionary coursework. It can be defined, across many dimensions, through your own insights and ideas. You are invited to pursue authentic personal change through your intimate personal ideas and your essential local experiences as your primary self. I am here for you. And all of this, only and ever - if it serves you.

Violence and Belief

I want to take a moment to distinguish between strong, bold action and violence itself. There are those who feel violence is necessary in our world. However, I believe they are conflating strong behavior, even healthy aggressive behavior, with violence. For example, an individual may choose to express themselves through a piece of writing which includes strong themes which are bold and declarative. Is this boldness a sign of violence? The key aspect of violence is that it includes a form of violation. The idea of violence and violation, then, is that it transgresses something which should be held intact. For example, it degrades a person's essential dignity or violates the sanctity of their freedom to make their own choices. Aggression is a natural and healthy form of exploration and expression, while violation refers to some transgression which steps outside the bounds of appropriate evolutionary conduct. We will talk about this more in chapter 8, when we discuss ethics and optimal behavior. This specific idea is borrowed from the Seth material, and I found this distinction - "aggression" as healthy and natural versus the avoidable violations of "violence" - to be helpful.

With that said, I want to discuss a bit about our beliefs and our tendencies toward forms of violence. Where do they come from? Why do we feel the way we do today? And what is the source of this violence? What should we do with the violence which is already present within ourselves?

I do not claim to know all the fundamental forces that have driven violence in our world. In a general sense, though, I consider it to be a symptom of a relatively immature humanity. There are so many dynamics at play in our world which are presented to us as inevitable - the way political powers exploit people, the self-interest of local fiefdoms, the perennial tensions between different cultures, the tendency toward colonialist extractions of natural resources. These can seem almost like "the rules of the road" of our planet. But in fact these are not rules. *These are some of the behavioral patterns of our global population at a relative level of maturity.* When we 'grow up' a bit as a human race, we may look back at the behaviors we just discussed and see in stark clarity how preposterous they are. How needless. We will simply outgrow them at some point.

However, I want to go beyond this on the topic of beliefs. At the end of the day, beliefs are not merely repetitions of phrases that we hold in our minds which therefore dictate our behavior. Beliefs exist within a framework of concomitant worldviews, stories, biases, lived experiences, temperaments, feelings. One of the biggest factors at play in our beliefs is energy. Remember that energy was the first principle of our Multidimensional Lens. We are going to explore energy a good deal more and see how it can inform and reshape how we think about belief and behavior on a personal and collective level.

Belief and Energy

Energy is not merely an inert fluid that flows through our world. Energy is an underlying reflection and subtle *reality* to everything that exists. It interpermeates everything that exists physically, and it creates *interconnections* between different people and the events of their lives. Energy is, in many ways, very much alive.

As an underlying fluid of our reality, energy carries our thoughts, feelings, and emotions. Our tensions, preoccupations, and obsessions. It may exert a sense of peaceful calm which helps us maintain equilibrium; or instability, entropic patterning which can devastate a person's condition. All that we manifest, all that we express, renders itself comprehensively and continuously through our energies. We are always reflected and emitting, continuously, through our personal field of energies.

In this same way, the world around is also absorbing and sending out energies. People continuously produce energetic signals which tune their field of energies. When we read social media or the news or watch videos online, we are connecting with various energetic fields at once. We are connecting with the creators, the hosting platform, and other people experiencing and consuming that content. This is why we sometimes watch the news and feel completely overwhelmed with anxiety. While the information itself can be unsettling, sometimes we feel emotionally overwhelmed and affected in a way that is truly overpowering. In this case, we are usually connecting to a collective field of energy which is struggling in that way. It is not us per se, but the energies we are connecting to. And in the case of news, we will be mostly connecting to the other people who are consuming that news and are having such strong reactions. We pick up these reactions and begin to feel them ourselves. Even when we are aware that this is happening on an energetic level, it can be difficult to decouple ourselves from this intoxicating field of energy. (We will discuss techniques for this in the following 2 chapters).

In this same way that a person can be affected by an acute experience watching the news, we are similarly conditioned through our myriad energetic interactions in life. We are like fish swimming through many waters and currents - all of these fluids have their own unique characters, and as we pass through them they interact with our systems. We add our color to these fluids with our presence; and we are influenced by them in turn. Through the twists and turns of our journey across months and years into decades, we develop the complex, rich, and nuanced qualities of our energies; as well as our beliefs, ideas, biases, and the like. For this reason, it is important to expose ourselves to different fields of energy - in particular, if we are able to expose ourselves to *healthy and balanced fields of energy* on some regular basis, this can be instrumental for our growth.

What this all means is the behaviors and beliefs of our world are encoded and exist as a kind of 'living entity' in the energetic ecosystems of our world. People are constantly influenced and affected by this subterranean energy system. Just as a person may have a blocked or stagnant energy system which is able to be healed and resolved through acupuncture, tai chi, yoga, energy work (which we will discuss in the next chapter), our world has a collective energy system which we work to heal, grow, and develop.

From this standpoint, it is in fact far more important to look at how we contribute to *the energies of the world* than to focus in a single-minded way on physical actions and their apparent outcomes. Sometimes people want to make the world a better place, so they take part in conventional activist activities - protests, petitions, op-eds, and the like. But if you pay attention to the energies of some of these activities, they can - in some cases - have an energy which is full of violent coercions, resentment, and a somewhat stagnant character of energy. (Note I am not disparaging or discouraging healthy political activism; only highlighting a possible limitation we may identify with greater awareness of energy.) If we need to heal our collective energy body as a global species, how could we possibly make a constructive change with a violent energetic character? From this standpoint, we see it is so futile to leverage violent concepts to try to improve our world. Understanding energy, we see more clearly the wisdom of the famous quote by MLK: "Darkness cannot drive out darkness, only light can do that. Hate cannot drive out hate, only love can do that." From a standpoint of energy, this makes perfect sense. Continuing the violence in our own quest for justice would be like playing different notes in the same key and tempo: the song remains basically unchanged. We have to change the whole song by changing our quality of energies.

This very notion - changing the game by changing our energies, finding a wholly different way to approach our journey of co-creation - is one of the main topics for the remainder of this book. One of the best ways to start is to learn some foundational ideas for understanding our energies and working with our energies (chapter 3); and improving our healthy energetic condition through key behaviors and insights (chapter 4).

Overcoming Fear of Energies

As we consider our energies as a medium for change in our world, we may limit ourselves by how we judge the world around us. Recognizing our interconnectedness with energy may cause us to feel avoidant or fearful of the world around us. We may feel vulnerable to threats or impacts from the outside world. We may feel that some spaces are impure and should be avoided. We may feel a need to divide the world up and reject certain things from us and from our lives. While I understand this point of view, I do encourage you to remain open to the things that happen to you and to the things you come across. I don't want you to feel powerless, because you are not. The feeling of fear *is itself an energy* that you do not need to emulate.

This is one of values of our mindset shift of the primary self - you are living your life, with your energy, and you are 'in the cockpit' of your existence. You have the power. You are strong, and you are in a rich place of interaction and experience. Please feel empowered to reach out and interact with your world around you. Feel empowered to evidence your care and affection toward others. And likewise accept others as fellows, people of dignity and worth just like I have told you that you are. The things that exist in our world are created by other people - sometimes these creations are relatively wise and honest, and sometimes more misguided. Let these things be exactly as they are, and don't feel prevented from extending your energies and your care to the world around you. You are strong and secure. There is a backdrop of clarity and peace from which we project ourselves into this sometimes strange world. So let us stay rooted in our sense of timelessness and be agents of care toward others.

3

ENERGY

T̶his is everything: energy and people.

OUR ENERGY FLOWS OUTWARD, manifesting our thoughts, feelings, and choices; and outside energy affects how we feel and act. Our energetic ecosystem presents a continuous, ongoing feedback mechanism.

Imagine that we are living in a computer simulation built on code (energy). We are constantly writing new code which changes how our environment looks and operates. At the same time, we are experiencing code that already exists from the past and present.

We are already living in this energetic world. We already have a relationship with it, but in many cases we have limited awareness of it. There is an opportunity to develop a more mature relationship with this dynamic and living reality. Understanding and working with energy opens a pathway to genuine healing, creation, and reformation of how our life and world operates.

Recognizing the Effect of Energies

Whether we are aware of it or not, the energies around us affect how we think and feel. For example, we may find there are some locations we visit where we feel tired, heavy, irritable, or uncomfortable. We may find it harder to think or reason. Or we may find it harder to express ourselves or be in touch with a sense of who we truly are in these situations. By being aware of energy, we can do three things.

First, we can note the extent to which these outcomes are related to the energies of the environment. We won't simply identify with the outcomes and believe it is "just us" or completely internal to ourselves. We will understand how the energy is affecting us, seeing that it is coming from outside - just like polluted air or a noisy room. In short we can **identify the energetic influence.**

Second, by being aware of the energy, we can gain greater understanding of why the energy is like that. What is at play? What is going on with that energy? We can glean some insights regarding the nature of the energy and how it is a reflection of the people who inhabit that space and their own habits. In general, the energy of a person's space is a reflection of their energetic character - that persistent quality of energy in that person which endures over many months and years. We can develop insights or theories of **the cause or source of those energies.**

Third, now being aware of how the energy is affecting us and seeing possibly some insight regarding why the energy is a particular way, we can begin to consider taking some action to address the energy in that space. Sometimes it means working with the energy of the space; sometimes we can develop a counter-thought to help neutralize the effect of the energies; and sometimes we just decide to go somewhere else.

Developing Energetic Proficiency

How do we develop ourselves to this point? How do we sense energies; understand their impact on us; reason why they might feel that way; and then determine productive options to address the energies? This is a gradual process of learning and growing, and it is more than life-long. I say more than life-long because we develop our discernment, judgment, insightfulness, sensitivity, and clarity over many personal experiences and even many physical lifetimes. Recall the second concept of the Multidimensional Lens: we are more than this physical life. Our capacities and qualities are not merely the result of this one physical lifetime. So, we will continually improve how we go about navigating and negotiating energies for a long time to come.

Still, there is tremendous opportunity to develop within one lifetime. And even if we have a proclivity toward working with energies in various respects and competencies, we will, to some degree, 'start over' in each lifetime. A fun analogue to this is a genre of video game called a 'roguelite'. In a roguelite, your character undertakes a difficult adventure and eventually dies, causing you to lose all your resources, gold, and skills. However, when you start over, you retain subtle capabilities from your previous run - your spells are a tad stronger or you gain a bit more experience from each battle. Similarly, we as people 'restart' each life needing to re-learn basic skills, such as walking, speaking, reading. But many of our fundamental qualities - how we understand ourselves and our world, how we interact with others, how we grow - continue to develop from across lifetimes, giving us the opportunity to go further, reach new heights, and explore new realities.

In this same respect, we have to 'recover' some of our ability or proficiency with energy in each life. In so doing, we refine our more 'timeless' capacities for working with energy.

In general, we can develop our energies through four main domains of experience:

Energy Work - the ability to mobilize or maneuver our energies, cultivated by such practices as direct energy work, tai chi, qigong, or yoga. Note that these practices may develop different qualities of energetic proficiency, especially depending on how they are used. If an individual does power yoga for primarily fitness reasons, they will reap the benefit of energetic health by virtue of the poses, but they may not necessarily develop an advanced degree of energetic sensitivity or discernment through this practice alone.

Energy Observations - being aware of what is going on in our life and paying attention to the energies. Noting what we feel before, during, and after. Simply paying attention to the energies and developing experience through observation. Utilizing psychometry, or energy reading, to better understand and analyze the information embedded within different energy fields or signals.

Energy Applications - a sort of combination of energy work and energy observations, there are many ways to apply our energies in life in an attempt to heal, resolve, unblock, or develop things. Many times, we perform various forms of energy application without being consciously aware of the energy. For example, when we are journaling about deeply personal topics in order to better understand ourselves, we are often channeling and focusing our energies strongly, building a specialized field of energy around us, and often activating key chakras, such as our third eye chakra or crown chakra, in the effort to better understand our integral personal concerns.

Exchanging Ideas - by sharing our experiences with others, discussing, and listening to others' experience (whether live, recorded, or in written form - such as in this book) we are able to develop our context and parse energetic experiences in different and increasingly experienced ways.

Direct Energy Work

In this book and in my personal background experience, I have almost exclusively used direct energy work as my means toward energetic proficiency. While I have experimented with other practices, it was only intermittent and did not translate to a direct, global, transferable skill in working with energy in my personal history. However I did not go deep into these other practices, and tended to stick to direct energy.

Direct energy work, or direct energy, is the form of energy work that I use and that we teach through the non-profit I work with, Mosaic Wellness and Education. I am coining the term as such here just to have some term which is clear and communicates the idea. Direct energy focuses on mobilizing energy through and from our personal energetic system through application of personal will, effort, intention, choice. It does not involve breathing, imagination, or physical movements. A practitioner is welcome to use breathing, imagination, or physical movements if they find it benefits them and this is an area they want to explore. However, we don't proactively encourage these behaviors, because those of us who have been using direct energy for many years do not do these things and do not consider them to be necessary or even necessarily advisable for developing energetic proficiency.

Walkthrough: Send Energy Forward

So, let us begin with the simplest of direct energy exercises: sending energy forward. For this exercise, we will send waves of energy forward, to the space in front of us. You can start by sitting in a comfortable position. Please make sure you are not driving or doing anything that would require your full focus. In general, and especially for beginners, we recommend energy work only when we have the freedom to relax and allow ourselves to enter a slightly altered state.

Breathe normally and stay relaxed in a neutral position. We are going to begin sending waves of energy forward, for perhaps 1-5 seconds at a time, with a short break (say, another 1-5 seconds) between each wave. It may help to set a timer on your phone or computer. We will apply this exercise for two minutes - just enough time to change your life.

Now, at this moment:

- *Choose* to send a wave of energy forward from your whole body.
- Pause a couple seconds.
- *Exert your will* to send a wave of energy forward.
- Rest for a couple seconds.
- *Apply effort* to flow a wave forward.
- Take a moment.
- *Flex that choice* like a muscle to send energy forward.
- Pause before sending another wave.

Embody consistency and continue in this fashion for at least two minutes. If you want to explore further, you are welcome to do this for longer - say, five or even fifteen minutes.

Dealing with a Lack of Sensation

If you do not perceive any immediate, discernible sensation when working with energies, do not worry. This is quite normal, especially when starting out. Two developments will mitigate this over time. First, during any given session, we will find our momentary energetic sensitivity and flexibility develop *throughout* the session. Just like our physical body needs to warm up before we really get moving during exercise, our energy body benefits from some time to warm up before exerting a greater quantity of energy and allowing clearer and more vivid perceptions of the energy. Second, as you work with energy in a consistent manner over many weeks, months, and years, you will find you develop greater energetic sensitivity overall. However, especially in the beginning, this lack of immediate feedback in energy sensitivity can be a frustrating, if quite common, experience for practitioners.

Fortunately, there are ways to mitigate this frustration; here are some ideas that will help us to develop our resolve and perspective when applying this practice.

First, we can compare our condition before and after working with energy. How do we feel after the energy work, compared to before? Often, we feel more relaxed. More calm. We may find we can think more clearly. We may feel a bit more organic with ourselves - less artificial, less agitated, less fabricated. This last feeling is due to us recycling older, more stagnant energies from our field of energy. We replace them with fresh new energies that come from a more immediate, authentic place within each of us.

Second, we can mitigate this frustration by understanding that energy follows intention. Whether we feel the energy outright or not, we can rest assured that, as we apply our effort and intention, we are moving the energy. We are, indeed, doing the work, as long as we are genuinely applying a willful exertion of intention to send the energies forward.

Third, we can appreciate that direct energy work is training a somewhat foundational skill for us as the multidimensional people we are. *It is absolutely worth the time and investment.* Developing our sensitivity and understanding of energy is like learning to work with *prime* - learning to perceive and harness fundamental forces at play in our reality. This will allow us the opportunity to become more advanced human beings in how we approach every facet and scenario of life. We do not need to use our energetic proficiency in every area of life - but it is certainly an available capacity that we can leverage in every space of our life. It also speaks directly to the fabric of existence and interaction in the nonphysical world which exists beyond the physical one. If we want to prepare ourselves for every fortune (as the great philosopher Diogenes exhorted of us so many centuries ago), we can perhaps find few candidates more worthy than the development of our proficiency and experience with energies.

Fourth, last but certainly not least, I invite you to consider the aspects of energy work which are, indeed, fun, pleasurable, relaxing, and a form of play. As we continue through this chapter, we will discuss other ways of working with energy which are deeply personal, exploratory, and creative. Let us embrace this sense of play and fun when working with energy. The greatest development of skill occurs when we enter a flow state, when we are truly absorbed in the work that we are doing. When it consumes our interest and also gives us a sense of connection and pleasure. This is absolutely available as we work with energy. It may not be an immediate or automatic outcome, but it is certainly something that we can achieve with a small investment of time and practice and a mindset which is oriented toward this playful state of interaction with our experience.

Energy Perceptions

Now, what should you be perceiving? First, it is largely personal. As we are individuals, our energies have individual qualities and characters. We carry the multitude of past experiences from our multidimensional history across a swath of physical lifetimes. All of this influences how our energies operate and how they are predisposed to interact with the world around us. For this reason, people will perceive energies in unique and personal ways.

First, we can divide our *energy perceptions* into two main buckets. We can experience *energetic sensations* and *energetic feelings*. Both of these types of perceptions are fundamentally the same - it is our internal, subjective way of processing some energetic event that is occurring. The difference is in how we experience the event, based on the event itself but also based on how we are behaving, consciously or unconsciously, to predispose a particular kind of perception.

An energetic sensation is when we experience energies in a way that is *akin to* a physical experience. Common energetic sensations are feelings of heat or cold; a feeling of buzzing or vibrating; a sense of magnetic pulling or pushing; a prickling or tingling feeling; and less commonly, a feeling of sudden impact. These are typical sensations of energetic events taking place as we interact with energy or mobilize our own energy. However, we can also have energetic sensations related to our personal energy system, for example: discomfort, tension, or blockage; or corresponding release, relief, and opening.

An energetic feeling is an energetic experience processed in a more emotional or mental manner. Energetic feelings include the entire spectrum of human emotions, feelings, sentiments, and even thoughts and ideas. Joy, euphoria, equanimity, frustration, fear, fixation, and optimism are all experienced through the quality of energies and through our perception of them. In fact, many of the times that we feel these emotions, the experiences are themselves energetic in nature. One of the greatest realizations we make as we work with energy and come to understand it better is the extent to which our lived experiences are taking place on a deeply *energetic* level.

Energy sensations and feelings are not mutually exclusive experiences by any means, and we often experience them both simultaneously. For example, we may be working on some block or concern in the energies of our abdominal region, and in so doing feel simultaneously a sense of tightness or block (energy sensation) along with, perhaps, a feeling of fear or agitation (energetic feeling); as we continue to work with this block and resolve it through our application of will and creative exploration, we may feel a sense of release and opening (energy sensation) and a feeling of emotional relief, empowerment, gratitude, and euphoria (energy feeling).

Primary Direct Energy Exercises

To develop a solid command of the direct energy practice, we teach three foundational energy exercises. Each one has its own use cases and advisements on usage.

Sending Energy: this is the exercise we used earlier. We send energy out in a given direction from a particular area of the body. The most common method is sending energy out in all directions from all areas of the body. (Earlier, we sent energy forward, in order to make the energy movement itself a bit more intuitive and hopefully amplify the results for new practitioners). This can be used to unblock and clear our energy system. It can also be used to clear or clean or donate energies to a particular space or person. Please be aware that sending energy does create some energetic *coupling* or connection with your target. For this reason, we should be careful when sending energy out in an area with energies that may be imbalanced or something we would not want to connect with. However, we don't need to be fearful of this outcome, as it will typically just involve a bit of shorter-term intoxication, which will be resolved with time and perhaps some detox interventions (see Chapter 4).

A common question regarding sending energy is, "won't I run out of energy? What if I am not feeling energized?" We can think of our energy like the traffic in New York City. There is no shortage of it - in fact, usually we are much more congested than we would like to be. The majority of times that we feel sluggish are a consequence of having too much energy which is not mobilized or in a state of active expressive flow - like traffic which is sluggish as a result of congestion. If we release our excess energy and address blockages to remove the aggravations of energetic congestion, we will typically feel and operate better than before. There are times where we experience generalized energetic decompensation, a true lack of energy, but this is uncommon and typically follows a sustained period of focused energetic exertion. In these cases, I find that simply eating some food will cause us to replenish our denser energies once again.

Absorbing Energy: this is the same as sending energy, but in reverse. We apply effort and will to *draw energies in* to our energy system. Similar to sending energy, this technique connects us with the energies our environment - however, this factor is amplified with this exercise. Therefore, absorbing energy tends to be a less common technique; and we only use it when we are in a space of very good quality energy, such as nature, a park, or (perhaps) our home or bedroom.

Sweeping Energy: in this exercise, we flow our energies up and down between the top of our head and the bottom of our feet in a cohesive cyclical *sweep* through our energy system. We can start by focusing our attention in one area, such as the top of our head, to aggregate a ball of energy there; and then subsequently moving this ball through our body down and up. This can be a challenging technique to get the hang of, but it is deeply effective when practiced well. It has the capacity to readily resolve key points of blockage, fixation, congelation, and intoxication through our energy body. One of the most effective ways of working with energy I have experienced in life is to perform an energy sweep continuously for a full hour. The depth of unblocking and positive energetic disruption I experienced with this particular exercise has been, in some ways, unparalleled.

Energy Practice

I encourage you to explore these exercises and develop your own practice, at your own pace and in alignment with your own sense of what is right for you. Here are some suggestions and ideas for consideration.

It helps to have a plan of when and how much you want to work with energy. I say this because working with energy is almost an act of defiance in our world today. Our world tends to flow with an energetic current which is incongruent or even hostile to clear-headed multidimensional self-exploration. Remember in Chapter 2, we said that our societies and communities have their own energies which exert pressure as fields of energy. Working with energy tends to go against the grain of our world. So, if we do not commit to a plan, at least at first, we may easily forget, or find that something disrupts it, or - all too likely - we will decide that we just don't really want to do it that much, after all. I've been there. Having a plan helps us to ride the waves of turbulence.

In general, there are two main approaches to working with energy. The first approach is to work energy several times throughout the day, intermittently. Assuming that we move through many different spaces throughout our day, we can take a few minutes at different contexts throughout our day to work with energy. This ensures we remain connected to our energies and our subtle awareness irrespective of the energetic fields we come into contact with.

The other approach is to plan one or a few times each day to work with energy in a more dedicated fashion, similar to someone who meditates or prays at certain times each day. We may decide on one or two times and work with energy for a certain period - perhaps twenty or thirty or sixty minutes - to refresh ourselves and deepen our practice. In my personal experience, this approach has worked better.

So, what do we do during our energetic practice? Typically, we perform the sending energy exercise, the energy sweep exercise, or some combination of the two for the duration of time we are working energy. We can follow a regimented pattern or we can do things organically or intuitively. It's up to you.

I often find that the *first time* I work with energy in a day is the hardest by far. At the start of each day, my intentions may revert back to normal habits a bit; I may lose some of the energetic patterning imprinted by willful application of energy work.

That first solid session of energy work creates a strong signal in my energies - it says that I am working with energy, that I am a practitioner of energy, and that this is a part of my day. Once I establish this energetic signal, it clears a path in the energies of my day to continue working with energy as much as I need.

I also find that using a timer has been very helpful for me in training my energetic ability. I will open up the clock app on my phone and set as much time as I plan to work with energy. Then, I simply forget about everything else and work with energy in whatever way is best for me until the timer goes off. When I do not have a timer, I tend to get distracted - 'how long I have been working energy, how much time do I have left?' My success rate in completing my energetic exercises is far higher with the use of a timer.

Energetic Competencies

As we work with energy and develop our skillfulness with it, we will come to understand the richness and complexity of our energetic reality. In turn, we will notice certain areas where we excel, where our strengths are evident; and other scenarios where we have an opportunity to grow a great deal and develop abilities which are more nascent.

This is not meant to be an exhaustive list, and it could certainly be expanded. It reflects some of the general skills or proficiencies which a person can evidence and develop regarding their interaction with energies. These are based on my own experiences and insights and are somewhat adapted from previous curriculums I have worked with.

- Energetic Immunity - how consistently an individual avoids debilitating energetic infections or intoxications when interacting with different energetic signatures.
- Energetic Potency - the force with which an individual is able to project their energy or their expressions of energy.
- Energetic Discernment - the clarity with which an individual can perceive or identify ideas, insights, or associations when sensing energies. When this trait is applied, it is called "energy reading" or "psychometry".
- Energetic Confidence - the maintenance of one's own energetic signal in varying energetic contexts. This is a complex behavior with many factors, and a person's energetic confidence can manifest quite differently depending on the environment (for example, around certain people or certain positions of power).

- Energetic Dexterity - how nimbly an individual can tune their quality of energy to the specific needs of the moment.
- Energetic Self-Remediation - how effectively an individual can work on their own energies, resolving energetic couplings, intoxications, shorter term blockages, longer term energetic issues, and the like.
- Energetic Awareness - the general level of alertness or presence of mind that an individual has regarding their energies and the energies of their environment.
- Energetic Sociability - the ease with which an individual authentically connects with and supports other people using their energies.

These energetic competencies can be evaluated in terms of "stronger" or "weaker" for an individual; however, in many cases individuals will find that their competencies will be more or less effective depending on the specific scenarios or contexts. The intent of this list is to develop self-awareness and identify opportunities to grow; attempting to maximize all of these competencies may or may not be realistic.

Note that these proficiencies are not limited to those who work with energies explicitly. Many of us leverage these skills *implicitly* in response to the demands of our lives. For example, a schoolteacher who needs to maintain a strong presence over their class may express a great deal of energetic potency from time to time; and someone who engages in expressive creative outlets may apply their energetic discernment as they strive to unpack the contents of their semi-conscious intuitive inspiration.

Living with Energy

One of the biggest reasons we would benefit from studying and working with energy directly is because we are already living an energetic existence. Perhaps most of how we operate through the day is in fact accomplished through our energies. Our thoughts, our emotions, our subtle perceptions, our choices are all rendered through the matrix of our personal energy network.

We live our lives enmeshed with the quality of our own energies. Just as the condition of our physical body influences so much of how we feel and act, our energy body's condition predisposes our life experience in many ways.

Following this, there are fields of energy associated with our behavior, our habits, our activities throughout the day. We cultivate fields of energy throughout our lives, in our homes, at work, in our relationships, which presuppose specific dynamics and outcomes. In a sense, these energetic patterns at play in our lives act as a kind of machinery propelling us to continue the behaviors we have presented in the past. Understanding and working with energy will allow us to better identify and make sense of these energetic patterns; and to take the appropriate corrective action to refresh and renew these patterns, if we so choose.

To state succinctly a rather fundamental perspective of life: *we are experiencing a life of energy that we co-create in partnership with our life, our world, and our people.* This concept makes me think about some common complaints about life: people wish they had more money, more success, more freedom. While these are significant factors and can make a difference, I want to direct our imagination to the energetic realities of these outcomes. If a person has these desires met, does that necessarily imply anything about the quality of their energy? If we find ourselves with great wealth or social status, we may find ourselves in the company of people who are more prone to insincerity, to exploitative behaviors, or to the general sense of malaise or meaninglessness that can accompany a life where the world no longer asks anything of us.

As someone who has worked with energy for many years and experienced many facets and scenarios of energetic arrangement, I will tell you something that you likely already know and have experienced: *the greatest, most wonderful and redeeming experience of being alive is in fact an energetic one; and the most abject, miserable, entropic, imbalanced, even hellish experiences of life are also themselves energetic.* While I do not personally designate the existence of a singular 'heaven' or 'hell' location in our multidimensional reality, I will say that heavenly and hellish experiences are available, and they - like all human experiences - occur through fields and qualities of energy.

Given that our quality of energies and the fields of energy that we interact with determine so much of how we experience life, the question will naturally arise, how do we go about healing, maintaining, and enhancing the energies in our lives? This is the topic we will explore in the following chapter.

4

HYGIENE

To feel clear in our energies is a remarkable thing. To me, it is a bare sensation. My body is quiet. My thoughts are supple. My decisions move into clean space and take action. There is simplicity and efficacy.

THIS IS PERHAPS the chapter I was most excited to write. It is alternately the most exotic and the most normal. The most revolutionary and the most boring. This is the chapter about energetic hygiene — being clean, staying clean, and keeping our energies balanced throughout life. If this sounds boring, maybe it is. If it sounds critically life-changing, then I am glad you see that — it absolutely is. I find the ideas contained in this chapter can serve as a productive challenge to many commonplace spiritual or philosophical ideas which may be ripe for reconsideration.

It still amazes me what a difference these ideas make. I grew up with almost none of these concepts baked into me from the start. As the youngest of five kids whose parents divorced when I was seven, I spent a lot of time operating instinctively and independently, finding my own way through life. I did not default to many social norms regarding mental or physical hygiene or appropriateness. These are things that I learned, with time, through various channels; I came to understand their value through firsthand experience.

ENERGETIC HYGIENE REFERS to the way that we maintain and develop the quality of our energetic condition over time. It has many facets, because maintaining and developing the condition of our energies is a complex and personal matter.

Because our energies are interwoven with how we think, feel, and operate, our energetic hygiene informs how well we function, feel, and live. It influences our physical and mental health. It is the humble craftsman of consciousness evolution. More than ever, I feel our world is in need of a more informed appreciation for energetic hygiene.

Our energetic hygiene is composed of two major hemispheres: our structural hygiene and our mental/emotional hygiene. We can also consider how our hygiene extends outward, into our environments and our relationships. We will consider each of these in sequence.

Structural Hygiene

Structural hygiene refers to how we maintain our energies in a mechanical sense. It is about keeping our energies clean, mobilized, and healthy - similar to how we would take care of a car. It appears, in its own way, in every culture's emphasis on conventional cleanliness and hygiene.

Some qualities that generally reflect our structural hygiene are the liveliness of our energies; their suppleness and fluidity; and how clear and unblocked they are.

Physical Hygiene

Principally, our structural hygiene is maintained through physical hygiene: bathing, grooming, oral hygiene, wearing clean clothes. We can look back on occasions where we did not take care of our physical hygiene for a certain period of time - perhaps due to a light schedule or a low mood. We may recall that this deficit of physical hygiene left us feeling more sluggish, slow, or dull as a person. Perhaps we did not think as clearly. Perhaps we felt less motivated.

We can contrast this with a time where we chose to clean ourselves after residing in such a dull state: perhaps we hopped in the shower, washed ourselves, brushed and flossed our teeth, put on fresh clothes. After these actions, we likely felt renewed, sharpened, clarified. This is the effect of physical hygiene on our energetic hygiene - it renews and invigorates our state of energy and state of being.

An interesting parallel of physical hygiene is the practice of hydrotherapy, which has existed for centuries. Historically, it was a common remedy to submerge someone in water or run water over their body as a way to ease discomfort or promote healing. While we may not recognize it as such, I feel our standard routine of showering could be considered a regular application of hydrotherapy to our energetic system. Because of the naturally clear, flowing, conductive properties of water, physical contact with water is naturally therapeutic for our energetic system. For this reason, when I am struggling with an especially hard day, I will sometimes repeat to myself, "all good things begin with a shower."

Physical Activity

We can also maintain our structural hygiene through physical activity. By activating our bodies, we distribute vitalized energy throughout our energetic system. Our accelerated heartbeat floods our body with fresh oxygen, which helps to detox our system. Stretching and flexing our muscles helps to break up and recycle stagnant energy structures embedded in our body's tissue.

It may give you pause that I am equating activating our physical body with maintaining our energetic system. But these two entities are in fact deeply interwoven, and we can scarcely nurture one without caring for the other. Consider yoga, for example, which is structured as a physical activity, but is largely considered a practice of energetic and spiritual health.

Physical Health

The conventional precepts of physical health also apply to our energies. Regularly eat nourishing food, hydrate, move and stretch your body, get enough sleep - these standard healthy practices will likewise strengthen and nurture our energies.

In this same regard, any activities which would degrade our physical health and promote illness or pathology would likewise affect our energies, such as smoking or intoxication. When we come down with a sickness, such as a cold or flu, we may notice that our energies feel affected, blocked, and intoxicated, and that it is harder for us to work with our energies.

Energy Work

Energy work is an activity done with the intention of mobilizing or clearing our energies directly. It is often integrated with physical movement, as in tai chi, qigong, and yoga, for example. These three practices may look like plain physical exercises (and they do promote physical wellness) but they are also designed to improve the quality of one's energetic system.

In addition to these practices which hybridize physical and

energetic activity, there exists *direct energy work*, which mobilizes energy without corresponding physical movements. This is the style I am most familiar with, and it is the style I will use throughout this book. I appreciate that direct energy work fosters a *dedicated* relationship with the energy itself. It can grant the practitioner a nuanced and sophisticated understanding of energy with applications for a multitude of situations.

Mental/Emotional Hygiene

Mental/emotional hygiene refers to the *informational qualities* embedded in our energies, and how these qualities affect us. It concerns our thoughts, ideas, emotions, and attitudes. These qualities strongly influence our short- and long-term energetic states — partly through the energies themselves, and partly through the energetic affinities they create with outside energy fields and communities of individuals. All these dynamics coalesce to form a personal energetic ecology, a sort of living extension of our own organism which becomes a major facet of how we experience life.

All that we choose to think, do, believe, and feel comes from within us as multidimensional people. These choices register through the active and expressive *signal* of our energies. Our energetic signal is the quality or character of our energies at a moment in time — whatever we are 'broadcasting' to ourselves and to our world. Our thoughts, feelings, actions, even unconscious desires — all show up in our energetic signal at all times. In the multidimensional reality, there is no clear division between what we express and how we are. Our energetic signal emits through ourselves, our bodies, into our energetic field, and across to our relationships with others and the world. It is in a constant process of creating our lived reality.

In some ways, I imagine that we are all living in our own

individual caves, interacting with the world through various openings to the greater world outside. We are like fleshy volcanoes inside that cave and we are constantly spewing bacteria, lichen, insects, fabrics, fixtures, and forms into that space and beyond. While there is a greater, objective reality beyond the cave itself, we are engaged in such a deeply personal process of expressive creation that we are, in many senses, creating our lived reality.

So let us consider some examples. What kinds of thoughts and emotions are we *investing* into our personal ecology? These are not meant to be prescriptive, but exploratory; take with them what you will.

What do we *believe* about the world? How do we think the world works? How do we think other people operate? What values do we attribute to life and to people? Are we open to understanding things anew? Or do we adhere to fixed beliefs? All of the qualities of these beliefs and behaviors will color our energies and their corresponding outcomes.

What are our common *thoughts* in life? Are we repetitive? Do we condemn people or the world? Do we denigrate others as inferior? Do we lament our lives? Do we come back to the past again and again? Do we fixate on the hope that an outsider will appear to clean things up? Do our thoughts probe and examine our lives? Are we curious and open to possibilities and insight? All of these thoughts will shape our energies - their function and effect, sentiment and tone. Further, 'broadcasting' these thoughts in our energetic signal will connect us with nonphysical company that is resonant with these qualities.

Even our *emotions* can be an energetic choice. What feelings do we return to again and again? Is it almost a ritual? And do we still want it?

Mental/emotional hygiene is a sensitive topic because it deals with the kinds of thoughts and emotions we choose to embody. It involves the cultural mindsets we choose to explore and emulate. It even involves how we choose to feel and engage our emotions throughout our lives.

Developing a mature, sincere relationship with our mental/emotional hygiene naturally involves some inventory of our own cultural background. We may recognize certain styles of thinking, feeling, or acting that we wish to let go of. These are personal changes. They belong to you.

Environment Hygiene

Our energies also influence our broader reality by tuning the qualities of our environments. The way we think, feel, and act in our regular spaces - our bedroom, office, living room - fills these places with our energy, over time creating a sustained field of energetic character. Our habits therefore reinforce themselves in different spaces: we create energy fields reflective of our behavior in our environment, and that environment's field of energy predisposes that behavior in an ongoing feed-back loop.

Many of the prior concepts around structural hygiene apply to our spaces, as well. If we clean and organize our physical space, the energies will be clearer, as well. We can also directly work on the energies of our physical space through sending energies, and we may find it is easier to operate there afterward.

Personal Ecology

I want to say a bit about how our energies form a personal ecology. We emit thoughts, ideas, and emotions; and we exchange these with the world around us, as well. Through these processes, we create an ongoing and living tissue system around us in the form of our various energies, their intrinsic qualities and reactions, and their relationships. We can think of our energies as *extensions of the organism* - they are a part of the organism as surely as an appendage or a physical organ. To put it another way, our energy body is as true, as immediate, as impactful as our physical body. And similar to our physical body (but in fact to a much more extensive degree), we inform the behaviors, qualities, characteristics of our energies through our choices and modes of manifesting through life.

An *ecology* means a set of relationships between individuals and their environments. In the same way, our energy system, our energetic *tissue*, influences how we will think and feel, what we will connect to, and how we will connect to it. It can predispose us to mature and productive behaviors or less-mature, less-productive behaviors.

This is in many ways a revolutionary concept because it creates a *persistent statefulness* of our thoughts, behaviors, and conditions. Recognizing our energies and our personal ecology will help us to better understand the *landscape* of why our life works the way it does and how we can effectively take steps to improve our conditions in life and work towards the things we really do care about.

Intoxication

In a sense, energetic hygiene is about becoming free of energetic intoxication. There are different kinds of intoxication. It can be more standard and environmental - living our lives and going about our days naturally involves some amount of degradation, adulteration, or intoxication of our energetic system. This is akin to how we naturally become less physically clean over time and need to shower and groom ourselves to maintain our hygiene, comfort, and presentable condition.

Intoxication can also be more acute, caused by specific relationships, behaviors, links, patterns, and choices. When we become energetically intoxicated, we find that a certain chunk of our energetic system becomes attuned to a less balanced or less healthy quality of energies. We can think of this less-balanced chunk as a kind of 'anchor' weighing us down. Because the anchor is weighing us down, it makes it harder for us to think clearly or manifest in the way we might prefer. In fact, it may make it harder for us to even manifest our own thoughts or feel like ourselves. We may feel 'stuck' feeling like we are a different person, or feeling like we are stuck in a box not of our choosing. This is happening because a certain segment of our energetic body has become attuned to a frequency of energy that differs from our normal, organic, authentic quality of energy. The energy has taken on some slanted or stuck or inflexible quality.

When we become acutely intoxicated, there are numerous ways that we can be affected. Here are some key effects and categories of energetic intoxication.

1. Artificiality. Rather than being in tune with our authentic wants and desires in a holistic, integral fashion, intoxication conditions us to experience life as a more artificial version of ourselves. We see a dimming of our authentic thoughts and desires; and a strengthening of some more insincere, arbitrary, contrived impulses.

2. Suggestibility. We tend to become more impulsive, more fixated, more hypnotized by certain activities. More prone to binging or addictive behavior. Our energetic immunity drops as we can be more easily drawn in to other energetic patterns and frequencies that we may not normally partake in.

3. Reduction. Overall, our whole scope of manifestation is reduced, numbed, deadened. This can lead to feelings of frustration or agitation, as we may, on some level, feel that we genuinely want to

manifest more fully; yet we feel hemmed in by the limiting bindings of our own intoxication.

When I become acutely intoxicated, what amazes me is how aggravated all of my addictive behaviors become. I grab my phone much more compulsively, and it becomes (seemingly) impossible to tear myself away from a screen, almost as though I was physically bonded. I am steeped in the intoxication energies, and those energies contain a vector field which pulls me toward the objective of the intoxicant. In many cases, this arrangement leads to hypnotic extraction, a dynamic where our energies are consumed consciously or unconsciously by a less-balanced nonphysical person.

Intoxication goes hand-in-hand with extraction, because our intoxication predisposes us to behaviors that make our energies available to be siphoned off by nonphysicals who wish to consume our energy. These unfortunate nonphysicals look for energy that resonates with them enough that they can consume it. It is like a vector field - they need to imprint their energy into us which contains the signal akin to theirs. That signal contains what might be considered a vector field of multidimensional alignment.

Categories of Intoxication

Environmental Intoxication - typically mild, this is the normal intoxication resulting from interacting with the broader world around us. Going to work, going to a restaurant, running errands, taking a walk can all produce mild intoxication. In some cases, environments can make us acutely intoxicated if their energies are imbalanced in a more pronounced way, such as staying in the home of a person with significant emotional challenges.

Substance Intoxication - using any psychoactive substance, such as alcohol, tobacco, vaping, or drugs presents its own intoxicating qualities. The psychoactive quality causes physical changes which predispose our energies to shift in quality and connect with energy fields resonant with that activity and its effects.

Social Intoxication - being with one or more people and interacting deeply with them can provide its own form of intoxication as the group creates a shared field of energy. Not all group interactions predispose an intoxication, but being with others means sharing energies with them, and we may take on some of their less-balanced energies. If we hold to our lucidity and maintain an authentic field of energy, we can support them without becoming intoxicated; but if we allow our manifestation to diminish, we will be more likely to 'take on' their energies and become intoxicated. This also applies to group settings - some stronger examples are rowdy parties, groups who act less mature or lucid when they are together, or people that espouse heavily affected or inauthentic styles of behavior or interaction.

Media Intoxication - when we become intoxicated by media, we are typically connecting to a group field of energy with certain acute qualities. Because media presents a relatively uniform experience for all viewers / participants, this predisposes all viewers to become easily coupled energetically, as they are sharing very similar experiences for that duration. For example, some movies, TV media, or video games can come with a certain kind of feeling, and consuming this media causes us to immerse ourselves in that pool of energy of all people consuming it. More time-intensive media, such as TV news or social media, are also engineered to be compulsively consumed, which predisposes intoxication through that hypnotic dynamic. The most prominent example of media intoxication to me right now is the infectious quality of panic and anxiety that can be triggered by consuming news media, both TV news and social media.

Thought Intoxication - we can actually become intoxicated simply by thinking about certain ideas and connecting with energies and communities associated with those ideas. A strong example of this would be fantasizing about violence, conflict, or sex. There are numerous nonphysical people who are preoccupied with these and would resonate with someone who is manifesting these kinds of signals in their energy field. This would allow the nonphysical to connect to a strong energy which is resonant with their interests.

WHILE OUR WORLD has always had problems, challenges, and political mistreatment, I feel one source of agitation is the fact that news media today is not incentivized to help their viewers feel a sense of calm perspective or wise reassurance regarding the events of the world. Rather, presenting an ominous tone of uncertainty or danger predisposes people to continue watching the news media as they hunger for some kind of resolution. Ultimately, this kind of resolution rarely comes from the outside world - we will more likely find resolution in our personal wisdom and greater perspectives. This is one example that motivates this book's emphasis on *primary self*, *personal ideas*, and *local experience* - to find a healthy way to bring our power and investment back to our lives and give less of ourselves to unproductive fixations on global events. *Our personal ideas in the here and now make a difference.*

An interesting personal example of media intoxication: I recently finished a video game where your character is stuck in a time loop at the end of the universe, and after twenty-two minutes of play, you watch as the sun explodes and all the people and scenery around you become eviscerated in the supernova - before starting again. Because of this setting, the game had a deeply melancholic, hypnotic field of energy associated with it, and I wound up becoming quite intoxicated by playing it and connecting with that shared experience of all players. Interestingly, the game is a genuinely brilliant work of art and has won many awards; it is not a mindless game of violence. And yet, because of the emotional nuances of the experience and the group field of energy around it, I still became acutely intoxicated.

Detox

Following a period of mild or acute intoxication, we can take proactive measures to return ourselves to our normal baseline of energetic quality by detoxing. In general, detoxing consists of any of the behaviors that would normally promote energetic hygiene. In particular, the supporters of structural hygiene - physical hygiene, activity, energy work - are especially effective at disrupting the accumulated layers of stagnant energy which compose our state of energetic intoxication. In my personal case, I find that drinking water, taking a shower, getting physical activity, and performing energy work (if I have the wherewithal) are especially effective.

If we are coming off of an acute detox, it may be important to sever the energetic link to whatever was intoxicating us. If it was a piece of media, removing that from our space. If it was a person, trying to gain a bit of distance from them or creating a bit of energetic buffer from them by separating ourselves for a bit and sending energy to neutralize the link. If it is a particular idea or set of ideas, performing some mental hygiene by focusing on something else for a period of time - even just a walk or a bit of TV.

When performing a detox, we may find certain key physical symptoms occur, such as watering eyes, yawning, stretching, or even coughing.

One key practice I have for detoxifying myself is my 'daily unwind'. I spend fifty minutes before bed without any use of screens. I sit up in bed with a timer running and just hang out, not really talking or doing anything at all. I try to clear my mind and work energy as it feels appropriate. In a way, this is a simple, stripped-down form of meditation that helps me to decouple from any remaining energetic links or fixations in my energy field before going to bed. Following the fifty minutes, I am usually relaxed and unwound and going to sleep afterward is quite easy.

Nonphysical Company

Energetic hygiene is an especially key topic because of how it relates to our *nonphysical people*: those nonphysical people who are connected to our field of energy. These are regular people, like us, who are not in a physical lifetime and happen to be closer to us and share our energies at a given time. Nonphysical company is a regular fact of life. It is not special or unique or rare. We all naturally interact with nonphysical people by sharing energies with them and energetic exchanges with them.

I want to acknowledge that this idea may be disagreeable for some people; the notion that people continue to exist and interact with the physical world after death may sound farfetched or old-fashioned. In my experience, one of the most jarring multidimensional ideas for people to engage with is precisely this, that nonphysical people exist and our relationships with them have a strong influence on our lives. It can also be one of the most pivotal or transformative insights, if a person arrives at it organically and authentically. Wherever you are at with these ideas, I want to stay with you and accept your level of alignment or disagreement; feel free to stay with the text free from any coercions or expectations.

I have made the point that becoming a more mature co-creator with a multidimensional understanding of life on earth involves understanding how energy and energy fields influence the way the physical world operates and will continue to operate. In this same way, understanding and appreciating the role that nonphysical actors and communities play in how the world operates will similarly expand and develop an individual's understanding of how cultures, ideologies, patterns, and groups operate and continue to operate in our world.

On an individual level, there are many essential facets to how nonphysical company interacts with us, many of them speaking directly to the topic of energetic hygiene.

Who are these nonphysical people? In essence, they are the same as physical people. They are individuals, souls, personalities, who exist and operate in the nonphysical context rather than this physical one. They will (presumably) undergo rebirth into a new physical body in a new physical lifetime at some point; just like we will eventually undergo physical death and continue existence as nonphysical people one day.

Because they are not anchored in the strongly-typed structures of the physical body and physical dimension, nonphysical people have a somewhat wider spectrum of how they exist and operate. On the less-aware end of the spectrum, nonphysical people can be a bit like sleepwalkers with only a dim level of self-awareness. They may operate instinctively and hunger after certain qualities of energy that they crave. On the more-aware end of the spectrum, nonphysical people can be like a luminous, caring elder who helps to oversee and shepherd life on earth to a more balanced, harmonious condition through the pursuit of our own individual evolutionary courseworks of learning and self-development.

For the purposes of hygiene, we will focus a bit more on the lower end of the spectrum, as we may find our energetic intoxication more commonly entangled with these individuals who are less balanced, less healthy, less happy overall. As we learn to understand them and ourselves better, we will be in a better position to help ourselves and to assist them in transitioning to healthier, more balanced condition, as well.

Energetic Connection

How do we find ourselves connected with nonphysical people? How do they become a part of our nonphysical company?

Your energetic state exists in a feedback loop with your nonphysical company. The state of your energies will create a 'landing bed' for nonphysical people of certain characteristics. Specific signals will create a singular 'bridge' for a certain type of person to come through and connect. We are a vast and complex ecosystem unto ourselves. And yet our intention, our thought, our deliberateness allows us to swing strongly in different directions by allowing these associations to flourish.

So, if we engage certain thoughts or emotions, we can find ourselves connecting with individuals who resonate with that. Remember that our thoughts and emotions are 'broadcasted' as part of our energetic signals. So if we begin thinking hateful thoughts or have a sex fantasy or start re-living the past, we may attract individuals who would be interested in connecting and participating with this kind of energy. Who are these people? In some cases, they are nonphysical people who are already associated with our 'energetic family' or 'group karma' - those individuals who have a closer link to us through energetic affinity across various lifetimes and centuries of existence.

As we connect with nonphysical people, we may enter into a feedback loop. It is like inviting someone into your home. Perhaps you enjoy tasting whiskey, and you invite a whiskey club friend to your home. And then, if this person is a little more impulsive, you wind up connecting with them and you both wind up drinking more whiskey together than you had expected. This is how nonphysical company can operate - like a person connecting with you and creating a certain 'social momentum' to go further than you had intended. Perhaps there is a time in your life that you can look back on when you indulged or went further than you had planned or wanted to. And if you consider the quality of energies in that experience, you may perceive the possibility that there was some nonphysical company there participating in your momentum of excess. Perhaps you felt a tiny bit 'hypnotized' or more impulsive than you normally would. This is not 'bad' or scary or rare. This is highly normal, a regular occurrence in our world at its current level of maturity and multidimensional self-awareness.

I want to make the point that nonphysicals do not control us outright. We are ultimately the ones in control. *We control our energetic signal, which determines our energetic ecology, which enables or disables our nonphysical company.* So, the point here is not to demonize or ostracize nonphysical people. In fact, I like to embrace all nonphysical people as common humans and do what we can to help and uplift all of them as fellow people. However, by becoming more aware of their role and dynamic in influencing our state and patterns, we can develop a more mature understanding of our multidimensional reality and overcome some personal traits to become better, more realized versions of ourselves.

Energetic Infection

If we find ourselves immersed in an intoxicated state, we may find that some particular aspect of our intoxication becomes inflamed or aggravated, causing us to feel 'infected' by a certain quality of energy. Sometimes, this may cause us to be in a certain kind of mood for a certain period of time. Perhaps we get into a bad mood or feel fixated on some particular idea or set of ideas for some period of time. We may feel like we're not truly ourselves - our energies don't seem to be our own. I call this state 'energetic infection', because like a physical infection, there is some kind of infected energetic tissue which cannot be readily or easily resolved.

Conventionally, this is often considered to be an entangled relationship with a nonphysical person, where their energy (less balanced presumably) contaminates our energy and causes us to operate as a less ably functioning version of ourselves for some period of time.

In a way, this makes sense, because the energies don't seem to be ours - we don't feel like ourselves - so it makes sense that this is a contamination by an outside individual. However, there are other possibilities at play. At times, I used to go into a 'Dr. Hyde' kind of dark version of myself every few months. Certainly, this state involved become entangled with some less balanced nonphysical people (I believe any strong altered state that is not wholly balanced involves some entanglement with nonphysicals). However, this particular pattern I had was based in my own pattern of repressing and bottling up my negative emotions. Over time, these negative emotions and sentiments would become a sort of 'dark liquid reservoir' in the recesses of my energetic system, one that I wasn't fully aware of. Eventually, the dam would burst, and the dark emotions would overtake me for a period of time, rendering me a much darker, more negative version of myself. It is hard to know these things for sure, but this is my best understanding of this personal trait, and by understanding it this way and incorporating my negative emotions into my regular manifestation more regularly, I don't have these same dark funks in exactly the same way.

If we find ourselves energetically infected, we can follow the same protocols for detox listed earlier in the chapter. I will also reassure the readers not to panic if they feel that there is some nonphysical person involved in their field of energies. This is a very commonplace occurrence.

Energetic Impulse

Our nonphysical company can also impel us to act out in a certain way. For example, if we have or have had some habits which nonphysicals might enjoy participating in - smoking, eating sweets, browsing social media, watching videos (adult or otherwise) - they may 'send a message' that we should do this again in the future. They may even lean their energies into us and see if they can coerce us into doing this thing again, like a less-balanced friend who uses peer pressure to get us to continue to do something they enjoy.

This is one of the reasons certain habits can be hard to break. On top of the psychological and physiological structures which keep our habits in place, there are nonphysical, relational dynamics at play. Nonphysical individuals who want to continue participating in this habit with us will exert an influence on us to continue the pattern. They may even send us rationalizations or ideas: "just for one minute"; "don't think about it, just start"; "you deserve a break"; "it's not a big deal."

You may wonder why I am giving the example of less-healthy habits and not healthier habits, such as reading, exercising, or eating healthy. Well, we will assuredly connect with nonphysicals while doing healthy things, as well. The difference is that healthier activities will connect us with healthier nonphysical people in general. And healthier nonphysical people do not typically attempt to *coerce* others to do things. This is one reason why healthy habits can be a challenge to maintain while less-healthy habits seem to take on a mind of their own.

If we wish to change a habit and we find that nonphysicals are making it hard to change by exerting a pressure on us, we have a few tools at our disposal. First, if we truly commit to our choice to change our behavior on an internal and personal level, it will be harder for any outside influence to influence our actions. Second, we can continue to maintain our energetic hygiene through conventional means - working energy, staying physically clean, staying active - which will keep our overall energy field more balanced and shrink the 'window' which would allow these individuals to connect with us. Third, we can even send the message, in our energies, that we don't do this anymore. The same way we might have a sit-down talk with a friend of ours in the physical body if we want to discontinue a certain pattern with them, we can extend the same patient, thoughtful, humane, and courteous dialogue with our nonphysical company, just by sending out the message to that nonphysical person. After all, they are not a bad person - just someone who is a bit less balanced and likes to engage in an activity we may be outgrowing. We may be surprised by the results of this.

Energetic Extraction

Lastly, I want to talk about the idea that some nonphysical people try to gain access to our energy and siphon it into themselves. I call this process 'extraction'. Why do they want it? The simplest explanation is that they want to consume it the way that someone with an addiction wants to consume something. They crave stronger, more balanced energies because they aren't able to produce it themselves in their unfortunate, imbalanced condition. Rather than giving in to this dynamic, however, both parties would benefit more if we take back control of our energies and apply them constructively toward the pursuit of our wellbeing, our personal goals in life, and multidimensional evolution for ourselves and others.

Building upon the ideas of the previous two sections - energetic infection and energetic impulse - we may find ourselves conditioned into a semi-hypnotic state at times. It is during these times that we are more highly intoxicated, more hypnotized, that we may find our energies get extracted by some nonphysicals, leaving us more drained and intoxicated than before. From personal experience, I would say the main forms of extraction would typically involve any kind of behavior that could be considered addictive or a fixation. This would include drugs, alcohol, pornography, social media / doomscrolling, excessive news consumption, video gaming, online shopping, overeating, and excessive use of any phone apps. Typically extraction will be more common in isolated activities rather than group activities, since groups do not typically experience the kind of hypnotic, trance-like states where extraction is most amplified (although some do, including group versions of all the activities mentioned above). Interestingly, one can look at a list of addiction recovery groups and see that many of these groups involve behaviors that would be candidates for a kind of extraction.

As with the topic of energetic impulse above, we can look at the behavioral pattern in our life and seek out ways to disrupt it. On a personal example, I have struggled at times with fixation on sexual thoughts throughout life, and I feel that this was a common entry point for a nonphysical connection to drive some energetic extraction from me. How did I correct this? I had to mature and reframe my understandings of sex and intimacy; and come to understand better the energetic, emotional, and cognitive behaviors at play in my person that led me to a kind of affective lack and would predispose a fixation on sexual thoughts. Ultimately, my less-balanced nonphysical connections were in fact a smoke signal that led me to an area where I could reframe my understandings of human worth and improve my integral energetic health.

Cleanliness as a Virtue

It is interesting to note how energetic hygiene calls to mind the old idea from the Puritanical settlers of early Euro-American history. These individuals were focused on cleanliness as a kind of divine calling. While I doubt I would be happy living in such a community today (coming from a 300-plus year gap of culture), I have come to appreciate that their insistence on a sort of cleanliness may have been at least partly driven by an intuitive sense of how energetic hygiene imparts a quality of refinement to one's mental and spiritual state.

Escapism

Escapism is rather fundamental. I have a tremendous background in escapism - I am a bit of a *connoisseur* in escapist behaviors. I think escapism is one of the major forces at play in our world today, and it plays into many of the more complex and relevant dynamics affecting our energetic hygienes and personal ecologies.

At its core, escapism is about *turning away from life*. It is about being *unwilling to endure awareness* of the situations that life brings us. However, life is life. Life is an ongoing process of new experiences. Life is a continuous fluid of challenge and novelty - even mischief, as it subverts our expectations. We can never truly escape life. All we can do is dull our awareness or redirect our focus. *But life is still there, the situation remains, and we continue to career through the episode with all the inertia of our being.* So, at its core, overcoming escapism is about recognizing life, partnering with it, and continuing to connect our awareness and our energies with it.

As I write these words, I am coming down off a bad few days. I was quite unhappy and felt debilitated by my inability to focus on things, my tendency to 'act out' in addictive behaviors by using my phone and digital media. Today, I decided to go 'cold turkey' and engage no use of my phone, TV, or any screens which was not in service of some functional goal. I am not doing this to be self-punishing, but to help myself establish a space and a connection to my world around me in the form of energies. I am helping myself to break in a field of energies where I can feel relaxed and at home in my life. I am committing to this life in the present moment, and committing to finding a sense of place in it where I can persist myself and not need to run away, not need to turn away or *escape* the various pressures, stressors, or difficult energies or ideas of my life.

In doing so, I have gathered some personal ideas together which will help to embolden me and keep me focused on this current goal. I want to keep my spirits high and not feel like a piece of crap while working on cleaning up my situation. I offer these to you in case they are helpful lenses for understanding or reframing the issue of escapism in your life:

LIFE HAS AN HOURGLASS SHAPE. We can turn downward, to the bottom half, where we turn to darkness, a lack of awareness, and a more comfortable regression into a world more aligned with our comfort and our easier sense of self. Or, we can turn upward toward the more illuminated half, where we must practice trust, vulnerability, and authenticity.

It can be a challenging ion storm as we face upward, but we can still draw upon the comfort and security of the bottom half while facing the sometimes harsh lights above. In that facing upward, we are facing outside our simple, pre-determined ideas about ourselves and our lives, and it is thus an act of *otherness*. This is a central and challenging life dynamic, and there is no shame in how we engage it. We do not need to change. We do not 'need' to face upward toward the light. We can and should find our own ideas for navigating this reality.

Let our motivation and understanding be authentic and our own.

PITY THE LOST. When we are in escapism or intoxication, I call this being "lost". There is no shame in being lost. There is no need to punish or condemn those who are lost. "Pity the lost," I tell myself. We would all be so fortunate to be intimately connected to our most advanced inner ancestors, to have unflinching integrity and cohesive beautiful exchange with life. We would all be so fortunate, but we are not always like this. Pity the lost - especially ourselves - and extend them your gracious understanding.

EVERY CHALLENGE **we face is the right challenge for us.** Every moment in life is our moment. It pulses with the true and full expression of life. It does not matter if this situation seems like one we've already had in the past. Life does not repeat. Let us embrace the truth and reality of this moment. We are never bad. We are always on the edge of greatness. We're always on the edge of a breakthrough. Embrace the challenge, for it is presented to us with unfathomable care. This is our space to play, to explore, and to become something new and old.

AT THE HEART of our escapisms is a wish to retreat from life. Here are three short sentences which have helped me in the past:

- "Don't retreat from your life. Advance into it.
  Advance into your life."
- "You have to want to be alive. You have to really
  want it."

- "Face the sun and the shadows fall behind you." - Maori proverb.

Escapism falls into many categories. I am using the term loosely to refer to any activity on a physical or energetic level which decouples us from a state of being present in our lived momentary experience. Escapism is not categorically a bad thing — it can serve as useful distraction, exploration, or recreation during especially difficult times. But we often use escapism to avoid the natural discomforts of being present, and in these cases it becomes less conscious, more impulsive. Starting off with a decision that is only semi-conscious and loaded with an impulsive quality tunes our signal accordingly and puts us into greater alignment with less-balanced nonphysical people. This is one of the most common pathways to energetic extraction — escapism generates a relationship in which a nonphysical person feeds off our energies by virtue of our signal aligning more closely with theirs.

In considering our escapist patterns, there are two areas we can work with. The first is straightforward: if a behavior is causing our energetic and mental health to deteriorate, we can eliminate it outright. The second, more complex process is to learn what internal postures are driving our escapist behaviors in the first place. One pattern I have noticed in myself is a tendency to want to "cash out" when I am in a position of some resourcefulness. When I feel relaxed or have time or feel energized, I want to find a hedonistic outlet to enjoy this. This is a subtle but pervasive pattern which programs escapism into my core decision-making. By becoming aware of this, I could play with this dynamic and the energies around it and seek opportunities to constructively reprogram it.

Drugs

I have had some wonderful experiences using recreational drugs in my younger years, specifically cannabis and psilocybin mushrooms. Using drugs can give us a sensation that we are more connected, creative, and intuitive about life. They can facilitate a memorable and charged experience of transition and insight.

With that said, I do not generally recommend drug use as a *practice* for developing ourselves or enhancing our quality of life. In my experience, routine drug use does not often lead to positive personal change following the drug experience.

One reason is that drug use tends to operate in a sphere of escapism. The trip happens to us, we are not necessarily driving it. We are not necessarily in control, deciding to go forward through things, making decisions, or creating outcomes for ourselves. Therefore, as a learning experience, it may lack a certain amount of firepower when compared with a difficult conversation with a friend or relative; or a challenging experience where we are forced to take care of ourselves.

But furthermore, I want to call to attention the quality of energies associated with the drug use and the nonphysical people we are more likely to associate with as a result of it. When we use drugs, we will tend to attract and associate with nonphysical people who are associated with that particular drug culture. In this regard, using drugs may not be a purely neutral, personal psychoactive experience. In fact, it may be more like participating in a common cultural experience with common fields of energy.

In this regard, using the same physical drug in a different context may produce different energetic experiences. If you were to smoke cannabis as an indigenous person in the pre-Colombian era, you would connect with a different group of nonphysical people than if you smoked cannabis as a student living in Brooklyn (as one does).

Promiscuous Thoughts

We will do well to consider the bias of particular energy frequencies at play in our world. There are groupings of energy fields which resonate and preoccupy themselves with particular emotions, feelings, thoughts, and experiences. There exists a grouping of energy fields which are preoccupied with sexual encounters. When we think about sex, we should be mindful of the frequency of energy we produce. In some cases, our thoughts about sex act as an access beacon which allows individuals in these nonphysical spaces to come and connect with us.

So, let us denote: the Promiscuous. This refers to those individuals, that category of being, which persists beyond the gate of physical reality and continues to preoccupy themselves with human sexuality as an obsession and a pastime. In their entropic hunger for sexual energy, they seek out unsuspecting individuals in the physical who still possess that sexual energy they crave. Using powers of suggestion and by aligning their thoughts with the fantasies of the host, they forge an energetic connection which allows them to exert influence over the physical person. They will reinforce and even suggest images or ideas to further stimulate our desire. Following release, we may feel strange, drained, frustrated. It is likely that the sexual nonphysical has siphoned off a significant portion of our energetic release. Beyond this, they have created a pathway of energy which will make it easier for them to connect the next time.

I encourage us to name the Promiscuous as such and see the hold that they have on humanity. As is the case with religion or spirituality, perhaps sexuality likewise will require an individual journey of reflection and definition on the part of each individual. By decoupling from the Promiscuous, we get so much of our own energies back. We are more clear and can make decisions unencumbered by their heavy fixations. When you experience sex free of the Promiscuous, it has a natural, relaxed, earthy quality, like a peach eaten off the tree. And by enabling healthier energies, we grant ourselves the opportunity to assist others better - including the Promiscuous - in our time.

Baselines

At its core, hygiene is about establishing and maintaining a baseline of healthy energies, so that our state is relatively stable and harmonious over time. It is analogous to cultivating a healthy personal *ecosystem* of energies in our life. This is a positive goal to aspire to, and my own life has improved dramatically as I have become a stabler person and developed a stronger, more resilient baseline of energy. For many years, I almost had no baseline, because my energies and mood would fluctuate so strongly. I was routinely affected and overtaken by the factors of my environments, as is the case for many of us. Establishing a baseline was a major milestone for me; it represented a formation and revelation of who I was underneath the turbulence of erratic and uncontrolled energies.

With that said, simply encouraging people to establish a harmonious state of energies has some limitations. We grow in different ways, and our journeys of growth are rarely static or linear. We are dynamic creatures, and our lives are dramatic journeys at times. Through grief, mental health, self-discovery, transformation and evolution, we will not simply adhere to a linear baseline.

Even when life takes us through unpredictable turns and causes us to show up in myriad ways, we will be served by maintaining our baseline. Developing and strengthening our baseline of energies, sustaining our patterns and practices of hygiene, will strengthen and carry us through those turbulent periods. Our hygiene will allow us to face life's challenges with more clarity and authenticity, less clouded by the specter of intoxication. For certain transformations to occur, we must clean up our energies enough in the first place to allow those evolutionary opportunities to arise.

While hygiene helps us to establish and maintain a baseline, there are additional forces which will allow us to explore enhancements, developments, growth for our baseline. The first and most powerful is life itself as a force for our own education and learning. When we look at life this way, as an instructive organism, I use the term 'Evolutionary Coursework', which is the topic of the next chapter.

5

COURSEWORK

There is no greater victory than a bad day on a good path. This is the true inflection point. Savor the salt and earth. See through the haze to the fundamental behaviors you are uncovering for yourself. Abide, and clarity will arrive in her time.

For a long time, I called it my *life purpose*. What is my purpose? What should I do with my life? Am I meant to do something? Is there a hidden capacity within me which will inform a meaningful maturation and realization of my life? Over time, I've begun to use the term 'life purpose' interchangeably with 'evolutionary coursework'. This is how I've come to understand it - our life purpose is one and the same with our own evolutionary coursework. We are multidimensional people - we learn and grow in our interconnected panorama of reality.

∽

ON ONE LEVEL, *I was always obsessed with my life purpose. It was like living on the carapace of a giant hidden animal. What was it? What was I riding? Where was it taking me? I struggled with a sense of purpose for decades. I spoke openly about this with my amazing therapist in my early thirties, who would calmly and enthusiastically tell me that life does not have any meaning. "There is no life purpose." But I could not disabuse myself of this notion. I felt my purpose was alive somewhere within me. I could hear her breathing in the quiet of long afternoons when time stretched on beyond my understanding. My life purpose did not call, did not sing, did not holler. She just breathed. The gentle motion of her lungs tipped me off every second of my life.*

It was a source of great anxiety for some time. I had a heart like a wolf and my mind was a decent santoku knife. There was so much I could process in life, but it was so hard to align things in a way that felt right. I started my life in Cleveland (practically speaking), and rebelled against the thick air of this inland settlement. I needed to be out there, to see just who the hell I was when I threw myself against the scorching heat of humanity's ambitions. I needed to go to New York and fling myself into the crashing jaws of our cultural and spiritual hunger as a planet. I needed to turn myself inside out and scream and watch life's secretions emanate from the walls of the Capital. Who the hell was I?

I found little quarter as I found few people to match my disposition. A hunger, a dissatisfaction, matched with an adroit and capable educated background. Some sincere interest in leveraging something meaningful. You need to find those people who really match you somehow. And finally I found something - good enough. A group of spiritist lookalikes dyed in empirical garb. The Projectiologists, disciples of Vieira and of one another, working themselves into the night in the volunteers' office of midtown. Far too blunted, still; far too myopic; but doubtless these souls were indeed cooking with gas. And this is where I learned it. I found my partner who, like me, blunted her creativity working in a somewhat joyless enclave to serve this advanced spiritual good.

I had to take my time. This was a tempering process. I held my molten metal underground for decades. I was not ready for myself. I was not ready to bring my things into the world. I could not responsibly shepherd my intimate energies into the world in this holistic and meaningful fashion. It took time and I had to work on myself. I undertook many projects and endeavors. One time I had the clear perception, "commit to the IAC" - meaning, apply my energies to producing meaningful results within the flawed and somewhat unsatisfying system I was a part of. It was still the best I had at the moment, and I was not prepared to do better all on my own. I was able to learn and get crucial training in that school. I went through teacher training. I subducted myself into the bowels of this life's terrestrial training. I would keep molten meaning tucked into the bowels of the earth.

And now, here I am, seeing the mercury seeping to the surface. My time has come, in a sense. And I have to merely trust myself and trust this process. Reader, I tell you again and again - this is me. This is a process decades in the making. This is no lark and practically devoid of inspiration. This, my friend, is eruption in the purest sense of the world. Finally, liquid elixir soul is tasting air, and the subduction is nearing its end.

Was there another reality, a split happenstance, where I trusted myself enough to march my shit out to society sooner? Brother, I have no clue. I will say this - nothing came through as cogent as this before. I had to develop a second skeleton, in a sense - enough formulation and structure to reproduce, to create something outward with an internal integrity all its own. So many things to learn in order to make this outcrop work.

THE PURPOSE of life is a deeply complex and personal topic. And it is up to each of us to define our life in the way that is most sensible for our disposition and mindset. One of the things I've found is that living well, meeting our diverse personal needs, tends to address any underlying anxiety or unease around our sense of purpose. I believe we do have a purpose, each of us unique. *And* - I think it will emerge organically as an expression of our healthy and vibrant presence in our own lives.

There is a way of living which is self-evident, which generates meaning by its very nature, which can ease any uncertainty around life purpose itself. We wind up simply living well in a multidimensional flow of sorts. That's more or less what this chapter will be about. There are two main topics we will discuss - evaluating life purpose and purposeful living from an energetic standpoint; and evaluating life purpose as a personal syllabus of evolutionary coursework for this particular life.

Life Purpose as Energy

What is our life purpose? Logically, it should involve some kind of creative outcome which will make sense at the end of our life from a multidimensional point of view. So, let us consider this from a multidimensional view - what will matter, in the end? When we are ninety years old and we pass on and we look back on our life? What is the nature of the wealth that has substantiated and given merit to our years?

If we had personal eras of status, wealth, and success in society, will it matter to us? I think that the success itself will not matter as much as the meaning and the through-line of that success. How did we relate to it? We can rather easily imagine a kind of success which left us feeling alienated, frustrated, jaded. Some other success may be tied to a deeply personal process of growth and expression, which would leave us fulfilled. So it matters so much the *meaning* of our success.

But moreover, we can look at a deeper level of things. We can consider the energetic impact of our life and our behavior. What was our impact on the world around us? And how were we impacted, accordingly? How have our energies been developed and refined? What have we learned? The *energies* reveal the true nature of our life and its outcomes. And we see it for what it is: a forested and mountainous seascape with all of the choices and co-creations we made, energized by relationships and connections. And we see how we all came out the other end, better for it. It was, in fact, a dazzling creation. A painting in five dimensions. Reach in and touch a spire of pigment: enter and experience all the richness of life.

But like a great painting of the romantic period, our life was not merely painted with lilac, lime, and luminous. It harbors the whole suite of shades and hues of human experience. Life is a journey with its own rich crookedness, challenge, sadness. Where there was darkness, there was the possibility to redeem it and see it anew. To cast it again in light. But also to learn to love the dark itself.

Life is a great creation and expression. But in our developing realization of understanding ourselves and our reality, things become richer, freer, more open, but also more solid and workable. I am compelled to work through things in this way because it makes life more *interesting* and *comprehensible*.

Going Underground

There is a difference between doing something public which is supported by society; and doing something which is integral to your purpose as a multi-millennial human being. The former is visible and typically has obvious value or serves a public perception of value in some way. The latter is intensely personal. It may not reflect society's values. In some ways, you may wonder exactly how it serves your own values, since the work you do at the frontier of yourself may be highly intuitive and not something you can easily encapsulate or break down into words.

When we truly attend to our purpose as complex multidimensional beings, it can be emotionally, socially, spiritually difficult. When you are working on your deeper purpose, you will typically be aligning with a paradigm or framework of value which is not overtly represented in society. So, you may look weird. You may feel isolated. You may feel ashamed or saddened because people whom you love and respect do not like what you're doing. Those loved ones may not be able to make sense of how you are living your life.

It can happen that we wind up becoming outsiders, in a sense. Hopefully, we develop a sort of tribe or family of people who have a similar outlook and can understand our choices. But even then, there are times where we must go it alone in some sense. We have to go beyond the borders. We must try new things in uncertainty, without others to affirm each choice for us. If we did not do this, we would deprive ourselves the personal joy of discovery and exploration. This is an idea echoed in Colin Wilson's *The Outsider*, wherein he says, "Ask the Outsider what he ultimately wants, and he will admit he doesn't know. Why? Because he wants it instinctively, and it is not always possible to tell what your instincts are driving towards."

So this process of being outside of things, this tone of social alienation, I call *going underground*. I spent years underground, in many respects. I felt like I lived a dual life, like Superman and Clark Kent (as described in the movie "Kill Bill"). In my private life, I explored and shared powerful multidimensional ideas. But publicly, at work and chatting with friends and neighbors and colleagues, there was no place to discuss this. I could only share a subset of myself, and the most dynamic and alive ideas I had didn't get shared with most people.

So I am sharing that I have spent many years living different sorts of undergrounds. And I know the pain and challenge of being underground. But I also know that it is not *bad* or *wrong* to go underground. You may go underground for years or decades. The world may not understand you. But you can find your way back to your purpose, such that you find a sense of alignment between your disparate components. My hope in this text is, partly, to create an underground colony, so all of us in our underground-ness can find a common space to connect and co-create amid our own authentic underground-ness. And, hopefully, to co-create new cultural tones above ground so that we have a greater ease and ability to share ourselves with the world around us.

Evolutionary Curriculum

Over time, I have come to see that our lives are our evolutionary curriculum. And this is, to my soul, the best way to understand this life experience. It is deeply personal and encompassing and educational. And in our learning, our growing, our erudition and education, we make an impact outward and learn to be more exceptional people through our life experiences.

Our life is evolutionary curriculum, our multidimensional coursework. For me, this changes everything. It means that we are here for everyone and no-one. It means that we are always at play, always in touch with the soul of things, always at one with the essence of life, because we are always at the threshold of our next personal evolutionary stage. We are always moving onward.

By seeing the coursework at play, we are learning to see the world more inclusively, emphasizing the 'and' over the 'or' - not radicalizing ourselves in favor of divisive simplicity, but becoming tolerant of our bewildering breadth. We come to accept our muchness within and draw upon the opalescent span of our enormous water table. And we thereby refine our temperament - to cross-calibrate all those tunes of ourselves in one sweeping motion.

What We are Born With

In order to better make sense of our evolutionary coursework in this life, we can consider what we are bringing into this life. We can think about who we were before this life began. What was our condition? Who were we - as multidimensional people living out a series of existences?

We may have had some tendencies and proclivities. Maybe we tended to have lives where we predominated certain traits and behaviors. This life is an opportunity to expand our horizons, sometimes by giving ourselves the opportunity to develop key strengths that aren't totally natural for us. Sometimes, there are some wondrous chasms into our person where we simply haven't developed much. And while it can be emotionally and functionally challenging to work on these great dark precipices, it can be tremendously meaningful and open up novel possibilities for our future and our group's future.

Some of our most important traits that we bring into this life concern *how we treat others* and *how we work with others* in a myriad of contexts. We can think about how we treat those we deem less than ourselves; how we treat those we disagree with; how we treat our own families; how we treat our co-workers; and more. All these relationships are windows into understanding ourselves as people. But beyond this, *our relationships do persist across lifetimes.* Many of us have had the experience of talking to someone and feeling we knew them in some capacity in an earlier lifetime. We may say this figuratively, but it may be true in a literal sense.

So while this life is our evolutionary coursework, that also means developing our relationships and our maturity in how we build and enrich our relationships.

Big Teacher and Little Teacher

Life is a vessel for our evolutionary coursework. For this reason, I see life itself as the great teacher, the great source of wisdom that will help us grow into the best yet version of ourselves. I call life the Big Teacher to distinguish it from all the other people, books, ideas, and teachings we will encounter.

Other people are Little Teachers. They may share their personal ideas. They may share frameworks and philosophies and programs to help you develop in some particular ways. Some people will try to create a school of thought which is meant to be final, definitive, encompassing. "I will tell you how the world works, and I will tell you what you have to do to be a good person." However, no Little Teacher can truly do all of this for another person.

And we do not need to worry about devising all the answers for any other person. We can try to help others learn and grow, but ultimately each person's learning and growth will come through their relationship with life. This can be frustrating, because we sometimes take the issues of others onto our shoulders and wear them as our own. But realizing that life is the Big Teacher helps to alleviate some of our anxiety as we work to assist one another. We find the correct amount to assist others in their growth, but we also realize that our relationship with them is not their core, fundamental evolutionary relationship.

And we know that life will continue to offer up ongoing opportunities for everyone to see better their opportunities to grow and develop and express themselves in new and expanding ways.

That is why I say life is the Big Teacher and people are Little Teachers.

Phases of Life

Life has its phases. There are periods where you are learning different skills, developing your character, undergoing core experiences. As adults, we may tend to feel that an authentic and thoroughly personal life is available to us if only we could solidify some productive habits. But it is deeper than this. Your life is your Big Teacher, and she is looking out for you. Life is nourishing your multimillennial soul with critical curriculum.

As my experience above, I spent several years tolerating a certain creative frustration. It was not time for me to show my ideas to the world - it was time for me to learn. In this way, we sometimes discuss our life as unfolding in two major phases: as preparatory phase and an execution phase. During the preparatory phase, we are learning more about ourselves, developing our core capacities, and creating a foundation for ourselves. We are developing core ideas and insights which will allow us to build things. This is like a foundational phase.

Then, in the executive phase, we are drawing upon all of those resources we have developed for ourselves in order to deliver some evolutionary value to the world. We utilize our insights, skills, ideas, relationships, and the like. All of these things play together to allow us to make a difference in the lives of other people. We are more mature, more patient, more capable, more understanding. We are wiser and have a more effective compass for knowing what is the important or crucial way to approach this situation. What does it look like to create a meaningful or satisfying outcome, from a spiritual or multidimensional point of view? All of this comes with the experience afforded by completing our preparatory phase of life.

Note that we don't have to wait until this 'executive phase' in order to already begin making an impact on our world. And in some ways, this is a false distinction. We are always learning, and we are always making an impact on the world through our authentic presentation of who we are. At the same time, we can expect a certain relative amplification as we develop our manifestation to be more in alignment with who we are beyond this physical lifetime - as we become a truer representation of who we were and are within the more unbounded nonphysical context.

I don't know if I necessarily 'believe' in this preparatory phase versus the executive phase. However, it would be inauthentic if I did not share that my life truly felt this way. I have developed greater clarity in my feeling of myself over the years. I am like a nut climbing out through shell after shell. I am getting closer to the open air, and the air has gotten better each year. Each renovation has brought me closer to a more pure and clear expression of myself. And that clear expression of myself, of my energies and feelings and relationships, has been ultimately the core of the enjoyment within the scope of my life. In this way, I don't emphasize too much the outward manifestation of things - I try to be detached from outcomes. Because the cultivation of a carefully nurtured life for myself has been this ultimate joy. And this local power to create something uniquely ours is the strength and capability I want to confer to you.

Synchronicity and Tightness of Coupling

Many people have been influenced by Carl Jung's concept of 'synchronicity', which means that events in our world may occur due to a *thematic* causation rather than a merely physical one. Things may happen as reflections of a common underlying meaning, rather than only happening due to immediate preceding causes. For example, we may see a book on a friend's coffee table two hours after having a separate conversation about the exact same book; to explain this in physical terms may be futile. The book appeared in an *energetic correlation* with the prior conversation about it. Did one event cause the other, or did they both arise from a common underlying meaning? The exact mechanism at play is open to consideration, but the idea is clear that our life's events proceed *interwoven*. There is deeper structure to the events in our lives, binding our experiences like the deep grammar of our sentences and paragraphs.

We can then consider whether we see all our life events in life as tightly coupled or loosely coupled. There is a spectrum of options in how we see things. Do we see any correlation between events? Does anything happen for a reason? How consistently does our life interweave itself in this instructive journey of our evolution? This definition is a personal choice.

One idea that interests me is that our life is more tightly coupled when we believe it is more tightly coupled. If we look for meaning in all events in our lives, we tend to find them, and life will seem to 'bind together' more tightly in a myriad of ways.

A Story of a Tooth

This is a strange and funny story which came to me some years ago. It felt very powerful at the time, and still provides insight for me in terms of how we invest in this life as it is.

For years, I was stuck between worlds. I had this life that wasn't really expressing who I was the way I wanted. And in my mind, I would sojourn on many fantasies that were a truer expression of my desires. I wondered if I should be an actor, a writer, a speaker, something else. Something other than a mushroom dwelling in this local spiritual office where we struggled just to pay rent. Month after month, year after year. Hamstrung by a bloated, immovable curriculum and an out-of-touch culture. How could I make the life I wanted? Did I deserve a better life?

It was a challenging time and a truly remarkable lesson. Because what I learned was that this is a hard time. It was a hard experience. It was tough. I one time went into a very intuitive place mentally and thought this through - it was like I was trying to climb a mountain with my partner. We were trying to get up the mountain, and here was this huge impediment right in our way. Imposing and calcified. It is a Big Tooth, I thought. Blocking my path. With no purpose - maybe it could chew something in another context, but it was far too big and isolated to be effective.

And as I tried to climb over it, I found there was no way over it. I was stuck with this tooth. And even if I did climb over it, I would hike for another two hours and somehow wind up in that same spot. There was that tooth again. What was it? I had to let go, for a moment, of my ambitions. I had to let go of my dream to be at the top. To let go of this hierarchy in mind. And to simply be with this tooth. What was it, I did not know. Just spend some time with it.

So I paid attention to it. And I saw as I tended to it that my energy entered it like water. There was a process - not hiking, not ascending, not conquering, but something nurturing and humble and simple. I am giving my life force to this tooth. Ridiculous and hopeless tooth was getting my energy. But it did not feel bad. Somehow I felt a fondness for the tooth as I guided my energy into it. But how could some dead calcium receive fondly such energy? And even in its pattern of reception... I could tell there was more to this tooth than met the eye.

And somehow, at some point, I realized it was no tooth. *It was a seed all along*. And as I continued to tend to the tooth, I made my camp around it, spent time there. And said, "yes, fine, this is enough. This life is enough and this tooth is enough and I am here to care for it. And as fellow travelers come by we can sit and be here with this tooth together. And we can connect over it. How strange and silly and meaningless and impenetrable this tooth is. So here we are together." I learned to enjoy this process. I learned to accept that tooth.

And slowly that tooth began to soften its tone. It took on a bit of color. Like it was winding backward in time, toward a fuller time. And slowly, in its own time, the points of the tooth began to shift and spread out. The tooth began to open and take on its next role as a seedling. It became a birth-mother, such a producer of vines and tendrils and peculiar fruit. We climbed with the outcroppings of this seed. We grew with it and developed with it. Hell, that seed was a part of me all along. The part that I could never truly accept. And as strange and frustrating and immovable - when I nurtured it, it somehow became even more inevitable and unstoppable than I could ever imagine. Unstoppable like a hardy vine. Something worth tending to.

That tooth taught me as much as anything. As I write these lines, the seed yawns and emits a fragrance which lingers in the pages of this book.

Just a Dip in the Pool

This life is just one dip in the pool. We come in, we go out. There is so much unbounded life throughout existence. All of it is available for us, and we are creators and participants in the breadth of the seen and unseen universes. We don't need to be too hard on ourselves about this time period and this life. We can relax a bit and be easy on ourselves and others. Because this moment, in all its complexity and challenge, is a provisional arrangement - a set piece. Let us enjoy and embrace and utilize the play as it is today, as a learning laboratory. Knowing that tomorrow will always continue the storyline, bringing fresh heat to our souls.

Invest in your life, here. We can always explore the deep space of ideas or scenarios existing in the wild fabric of possibility. But there is something sacred about this moment, how all those "ifs" collapsed into this one actuality. These hands, this air. These people. This breath. When we connect this breath with this moment, when we truly inhabit the center fold of this life. This is when life softens and becomes receptive to the glimmering song of our co-creations.

Hygiene

We talked about hygiene in the last chapter, which refers to our ability to keep our energies clean and in a healthy, renewed state throughout our lives. This is particularly relevant to our evolutionary curriculum for a few reasons.

First, if we do not maintain some kind of energetic hygiene, our quality of energies will suffer as a result. And this means that our quality of thoughts and ideas, our general level of manifestation, our ability to perform, our ability to synthesize new ideas, our overall level of authenticity will all be diminished. If we consider our evolutionary curriculum to be a process of exploring and meaningfully going beyond the boundaries of our existing experiences, then being in a rather intoxicated or non-hygienic state will keep us recessed further within that sphere of personal experience, since in that state it is hard for us to even perform or process at our current optimal level. So, maintaining energetic hygiene gives us the best chance to engage our evolutionary curriculum in a meaningful way.

Second, hygiene plays heavily into the aforementioned idea around investing in your life here. **Investing in this life** means being open to this life. Listening to it, hearing it for what it is, being present with it. Giving it our heart, if only that it may take root and nourish the soil. If we can't do this, and instead reside in fantasies or escapist ideas, we will continually divest our energies *out* of this life. Our energies are thereby dispersed or (in many cases) subject to siphoning and extraction by imbalanced nonphysicals who partake in less-productive energy exchanges.

There is an additional aspect of energetic hygiene which ties into our evolutionary curriculum, and this comes in the form of long-lived energetic blocks or disturbances that exist in our energy body. As we work with energy and learn more about ourselves, we will find that there are some structures existing in our energetic body which can be worked out, resolved, or released. These could be areas where there is an energetic lack, like a sort of 'hollow' of energy; or they could be an area of blockage where the energy is stuck and stagnated and does not flow. These may be blocks that we were born with, perhaps reflecting a personal condition which predates our birth. In some cases, I have worked out blockages and felt like I was having a kind of sense-memory of a past life while it worked itself out. In any case, the presence of these energetic blocks or lacks can represent long-term achievements in our own condition which allow us to advance ourselves.

Note that, if we do resolve some energetic disturbance in our energy body, there is still the likelihood that it was reinforced by some subtle trait or behavior that we were manifesting in life. So, if we want to move past that disturbance for good and keep our energies in more healthy condition, we may need to gain a sense of what was causing that blockage in the first place and experiment with some small internal adjustments in our mentality, our postures, our thoughts, or our habits, in order to truly advance to a new state of energetic vibrancy.

ON THAT TOPIC of Investing In This Life, I want to mention that it is a typical thing for people to not recognize the value of the current moment. We may see other scenarios and experiences as more fundamental, more important, more real than this one. We may see this moment as boring, mundane, or an illusion. However, our life is in fact a kind of kaleidoscope of multidimensional experience, and this moment is as valuable and important as any other moment in life. While some moments may be more memorable or treasured for us for various reasons, or in fact a bit more pivotal for certain outcomes to occur, it is not the case that any moment is less important or real or valuable. So I invite you - here, now, and always - to be open to this moment. To invest in this moment. To care for this moment and love this moment. It will treat you well. And the more you tend to the plants in your garden - all the facets and fixtures of your life - your life's accoutrements will reward you with their own symbiotic flourishing.

When we invest in our life, we will be rewarded with beauty and vibrancy. In this way, our life is like a garden. We tend to our garden. To our plants. To all the people and things in our life. And by caring for them, we make our lives more rich and healthy. It is not about finding that specific escape hatch that will allow us to access a more meaningful life. Friend, we are already in the garden. Now, let us be present and at peace with our garden. Let us look around and pay it good company. Let us attend to these beings around us. Let us nourish them.

On that note, it is important and worthwhile to treat

everyone we know and meet as a manifestation of all of reality. Treat every single person as vital and essential and fundamental. Because they are. We will discuss this further in the following chapter on Otherness.

Fresh and Pertinent Challenges

Our lives exist in this tapestry of synchronicity. Time weaves us in her meaning. The multidimensional spectrum of our life experience is in fact a personalized curation for our own evolutionary curriculum. What this means is that we live life constantly on the edges of our experience, on the edges of our past knowledge and education. We are experiencing challenges which are always new.

Even when we find ourselves repeating the same activity throughout life, we need not be fooled into thinking it is the same. Of course Heraclitus said, "you cannot step into the same river twice". We become agitated and stressed sometimes thinking that we are in a repetition. When we feel we have had a setback and we have to fix the same mess again and again. This sense of repetition can be overwhelming, and we begin to feel that we live in a life devoid of meaning. Even a single hour, a single minute devoid of meaning can be enough to desiccate the soul of a man. Let us rebuke such a notion. All moments are charged, bubbles of experience upon the very sea of meaning. Every challenge is the fresh challenge. Every breath is at the edge of our experience. We are always touching something real, for we are never detached from our indomitable, our multidimensional core.

Life affords us an endless breeze of new and expanding experience.

Understanding Your Life Purpose

People want to understand their life purpose. I don't think it is just a nut to crack, however. There is no fortune inside telling you to be this profession or start that organization. It is something deeper and more pervasive.

Understanding your life purpose is a process of investing in the world around you. Taking care of the things that exist around you. And finding those things that are interesting to you and exploring them. But also staying healthy and balanced in your life. Maintaining your wellness in all its many pieces. And along the way, you will find your areas of interest and explore them accordingly.

Your life purpose is not an identity. Your identity is a sense of who you are, which is developed slowly and tectonically. It is a geological entity. You do not need to reinvent yourself. You can do so, feel free to do so, but you do not need to recreate yourself as some entity to jump into. You are a dark planet and you can explore those nascent energies dwelling in the mystery of your terrain.

When I have let go of my hangups and I feel seated within a living shroud of co-creation, I think to myself: we are undiscovered lands.

Nascent Personal Energies

To a certain degree, our life purpose is embedded in the intimacy of our souls. **We are harboring deep and subtle energies within us which house the meaning of our life purpose.** It is latent within us, coloring all we do, and coming outward as an expression. As we express our energetic signal, we can find those spaces and opportunities to allow our more intimate, internal ideas to come through, allowing our nascent personal energies to come through. This relates back to our idea in Chapter 1 of Personal Ideas.

One of the most common mistakes we make is to look at our life and see our purpose as a rather trivial outward action. Writing a book, starting a company, having a career. All these things can be urgent and important, but the essence of our life purpose is our own edification and growth and maturation. Our evolutionary coursework.

Our life purpose, rendered through our evolutionary coursework, is a process of unfolding, developing, refining, and maturing ourselves integrally as multidimensional beings. While we may look at the world around us and all the issues which seem incredibly urgent, we should remember that this world is a product of the collective psyche at play in the broader multidimensional reality of our moment. The world is not as it is by accident. The world is, in many respects, a *choice* made by the collective. Just as we should not override the free will of another, we also do not need to override the collective free will and attempt to violently reshape the world into our image. Instead, we can form our strong relationships with others, create meaningful exchange, and allow ourselves and others to correct our ways incrementally and create new possibilities for this world.

Letting go of a global reference and embracing our *local experience*, as we discussed in Chapter 1, allows us to recognize the full validity of our individual experience and process of living. By being fully invested in our lives, we are able to truly subvert the institutionalized pains of the world by rewriting our local rules with our equanimous energy. "What the world needs is people who have come alive."

Not Just One Thing

The world is not just one thing. We are tempted to look at large-scale global events and collapse the breathtaking panorama of multilayered life into fixed conversations about economic topics. But in truth, life is, and has always been, so very rich, so very huge. Let us look upon it as a dark map with currents of blue meaning coursing through the thicket. Life and our coursework involves us tapping into that meaning and bringing it into our lives. We learn to be more adept and adroit in resonating that true and deeper meaning into being. Not just a news article or an op-ed: a multidimensional relationship with our local, lived experiences.

Life is not just one thing. We are tempted to think of our life as a purpose. Steve Jobs had Apple. Beethoven had his compositions. Stephen King has his books. We think about the creations and see life's purpose in the creation of outward artefacts for others to experience. We feel the need to substantiate or translate our own being into something outside of ourselves. Otherwise, we don't feel we are valid. We don't feel we are real, as though we never deserved to be.

But this is a mistake. Our multidimensional fabric of reality transcends time and space. We are already our great artistic creation - here in this moment. There is no finer human creation than the transcendence, the infinitude in the drop of a moment shared between two people. Just sharing a moment together. This is not something to be outdone by anything, anywhere, ever.

Interestingly, Stephen King shared a similar turn of mindset in his book, "On Writing". At first he kept his writing desk in the center of his office, commanding the space. Over time, he realized he had been affording it too much status, and moved it to the wall, because your writing exists to support your life - not the other way around. And so, our great works are interwoven with our evolutionary coursework. We are not in subservience toward our works. We are not doing acts of service. We are growing and learning and enmeshing ourselves in this great interdependent web of development.

Victimhood

One of the most prevalent mindsets I struggle with personally is the tendency to look at my life as a victim. If I feel overfull after dinner and get grouchy, or if I am out of sorts on the weekend, or if I am having a bad day, I tend to posture my whole self toward the world as if somebody else did this to me. In fact, we are in an ongoing dynamic relationship with our world. We are like a knife with her tongue against the whetstone. We are in a position to refine ourselves continually through the curated choices of life. We are in the fulcrum of essential personal change.

The world is complex and there are many theoretical concepts around recognizing oppression and seeking justice in this global society. I seek to validate these points of view while simultaneously standing in the truth of my personal idea as follows: "in all ways reasonable, let us disabuse ourselves of any notion that we are victims." Let us partner with life in every way possible. Let us put our imaginations to work to understand *how* all our challenges (great and small) may be understood as our evolutionary coursework at play.

Writing Space

One of the best ways to develop and explore our nascent personal energies is through the practice of writing. When we write, we create a curated field of energy dedicated to our task of unpacking, exploring, understanding. We can channel our intentions and bring out deeper intuitions from within us. This allows us to activate and relate with our own ongoing unfolding. When I write, I feel the apparent truthfulness of the phrase, "ask and you shall receive."

When we write and create in this way, it is not merely a matter of imitating those around us. And yet, there is a mimesis which is essential. In life, we exchange energies with others and learn from them and, in some senses, render our own versions of their outputs. Our written works are inspired by those other works we have read. This exchange and renewed personal creation is a valid and meaningful part of life. We aren't meant to do it all on our own. But we are meant to make it *ours*.

In addition to writing, we can create a dedicated space for any particular purpose. And by creating that dedication of space, we create a specialized field of energy which will channel and accelerate our ability to deliver on those intentions.

Maturity

One of the best ways to understand our course of life as individuals and as a planet is to consider what it means to mature. We can consider an extended analogy. In a given life, a person starts life with little awareness of all the complexities, nuances, and ambiguity that life entails. They also may not be able to regulate their emotions or behavior as well as they will when they reach an older age. As a person grows and matures in life, they have powerful experiences over time which teach them crucial lessons. And their wisdom accumulates over days, months, years. Their life becomes more complex and nuanced, and if they are able to navigate their lives in a fortunate manner, they wind up rather satisfied with life and gain a certain perspective of things which gives them a sense of security and clarity.

We can think of our own multidimensional maturity in a

similar way. Looking at our world, how would we evaluate our maturity? In some respects, I think the maturity of our planet is better than we give it credit for. We have managed to co-create a massive global economy where people contribute based on their interests, skills, and affinities, and create opportunities for a great many individuals. The development of technology, of travel, of educational programs, has allowed the scope of experience available to us in a given life to expand massively.

On the other hand, we have a lot of room for growth as a planet. We wonder why our world works the way it does. Why do we continue to wage war; why can it be so hard to eke out a living; why is there so much acrimonious division in our political world. All of these challenges are symptoms of a relatively immature world. So, I don't think we need to panic. Things can feel scary and overwhelming at times. I agree. But I remember that we have been pursuing this civilization experiment as a species for several millennia now, and there have been many states and governments of varying quality and style. We are learning and working things out. But we are still in our awkward years. Perhaps we are in a kind of 'middle school' phase. And I lovingly, jokingly refer to middle schoolers as 'the worst of everything that humanity has to offer'.

We can calm our nerves a bit, because the world has struggled for a long time. In the preceding century, we had several terrible, awful wars which claimed tens of millions of people. The Soviet Union alone lost twenty-seven million souls in World War II - nineteen of them civilians. In this twenty-first century, we are seeing some painful and disconcerting things. And yet, let us place the horrors of the twentieth century on one side of the scale and see what is still better before us.

But I also remember that our world is, I tell myself, a projection of our collective psyche. And as soon as we are ready to move past these things and advance ourselves to a higher plane of coursework, we can graduate as a planet. Let's work on ourselves and dedicate ourselves to the meaningful humanitarian work which is endemic to our ethics as multidimensional people. And we can do our part to build a better world for ourselves and others.

We are All Enmeshed

We are all enmeshed in our coursework. It is always bringing these issues into our faces at some regular interval. I don't care how much wealth or status a person has - they are in the game as well, and they are also players in the process of personal challenge. They are not exempt, and we cannot escape it. We can choose to hide from it, but this only serves to dim the true joy and satisfaction from life - the true fullness that comes from exploring and engaging our evolutionary coursework.

Sometimes, I hit traffic when I want to move. I have to sit with something when I'd rather not. And I think to myself: life is bringing the issue right up into my face. It is affording me a powerful proximity. It is allowing me an intimacy of space with myself and my own challenges. I will apply my imagination to see how I am not a victim; how this moment is a new challenge; and how life is my Big Teacher and my partner. How she helps me to move through the mountains like a music.

Paths of Life

There are many paths through life. To make sense of it, we collapse the totality of our lives into narrow, literal pathways. Many of them involve career development, wealth development, achievement of status. What strikes me is how people can give themselves over to achieving these things and find themselves unfulfilled with it. And I look at the things that truly made me happy - community, meaningful engagement, connections. Being part of a group. Creative expression. Now, I am also proud of my development in terms of career and profession. These things have been very important for me. But I also remember how a person can isolate themselves through a pure pursuit of the default paths in life: job to wealth and status to retirement. Finally, all alone.

Sometimes these paths are a way of learning to be unhappy. I tell myself, believe in your burgeoning creative expression of values. Challenge yourself - challenge your intelligence - to innovate what an amazing life looks like. Activate dormant crystals in the central chamber. Have all those things that bring you wonder, belonging, and fulfillment. You are the Artist. Now let's have it.

6

OTHERS

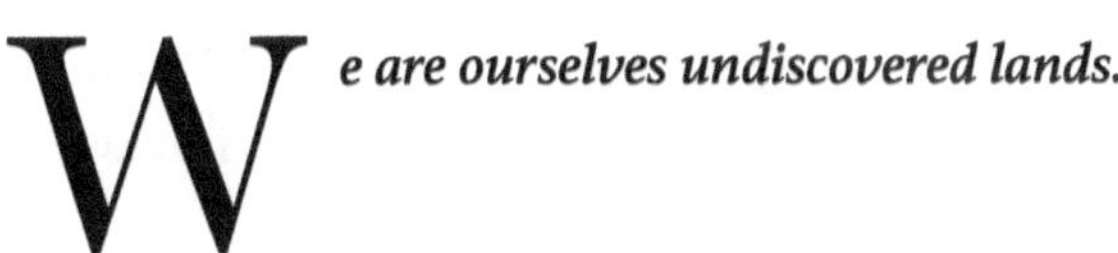

WE EXIST in relationship - with ourselves, with others, with our world. Our relationships are ecosystems of ideas, experiences, and transactions.

Our relationship with others - our Otherness, in a literal and figurative sense - is highly complex. Sometimes we are faced with something that is new to us, but we reframe it mentally and force it into a box of something we already know and understand. We take the other and rewrite it into a compartment of our self, breaking the power of its authentic otherness.

The identity can act like a distortion field, warping all things into the limited vocabulary of your personal universe. When we are introduced to a new idea of virtue, we may presume we already embody this virtue and then make middling examples to support this. Here, we fail to step out and meet the other, authentically, naked in what we are.

Others are our great challenge, but they are our great opportunity. Without the other, we would be forever in a cave watching shadow forms dancing in dimness. The other brings us out into space, even to the hardcore fogs of ozone that make our skins burn. The other is where life may come in cold and hard and dark. It calls upon our imagination and resilience to see the partnership of life sitting in there, curved and dormant like a stranger's hand in nighttime's still indigo.

Otherness

What do we mean when we talk about Otherness? Otherness means our experiences, practices, characteristics, and behaviors when we encounter things outside of our selves. But what is the 'self'? It can mean many things.

From the perspective of Otherness, the 'self' is squishy and malleable. It refers to all the ideas, senses, cultures, actions, touchpoints, feelings, intonations, attitudes, aesthetics, and preferences which are closer to our immediate sense of who we are and what our life is. It is that fuzzy region of all those things that are closer to us. The region of the self contains things that, typically, are less challenging for us and allow us to maintain a comfortable inertia in our life. In general, it means those things that are familiar to us and the things that we welcome into our lives. It is those things we deem acceptable.

Others, accordingly, fall into many buckets. They can be other people; challenging experiences; new ideas and perspectives; different cultures; tastes and aesthetics which are not familiar to us; emotions and facets of ourselves that we tend to repress; and many things that are uncomfortable, disorienting, or unfamiliar for us.

Otherness, then, is an experience of encountering something beyond ourselves which resides a bit further out from ourselves. How do we treat it? If the self is typically the abode of those things we find acceptable, then experiences of others are typically met with a kind of rejection. We find it hard to accept the other. We will need to transform it into something we can understand, if it's something not immediately sensible to us. If it is a difficult experience, we may respond by claiming this is an unfair experience, something we should not have to put up with. If it is something we strongly disagree with, we may become a storm of bluster condemning all those things that are so far from our values - we would wish to destroy these other ideas and eradicate this other from our lives.

The practice of Otherness, then, is developing how we respond to these experiences. When we are confronted with Others, how do we respond? As we develop our practice of Otherness, we may find that our own domain of tolerance and comfort begins to expand. We also develop some musculature, some skills which allow us to work with the Others as they enter our reality. We learn to say, "yes, this is right for me" - even if it is not something we can make sense of. Can we look the strange creature in the eye? Can we embrace the alien? And say, "welcome, brother, for I know that we are meant to be here together."

As we explore and develop our Otherness, we will tend to cultivate a personal attitude of *willingness*. When facing the Other, we cannot claim mastery or absolute power over the situation. We are in a complex, nuanced arrangement. We have to show up with who we are and just do our best. What we can do is extend our *willingness*: say that we are willing to be present with the situation and give ourselves to this experience at hand. Each experience we have - especially if it is an experience of Otherness - is a rich, dynamic crucible of evolutionary power. If we can reach into it, we can make an evolutionary benefit of any experience. Developing relationships, gaining insights, cultivating the garden. Making delights for ourselves and our loved ones. This happens, slowly and quickly in its time, when we extend ourselves in a posture of willingness to the challenges that life presents to us.

Powerlessness and the Shadow

I mentioned that we are not fully in power in our Otherness. And this is perhaps the part of it that is most challenging for people. In many ways, our societies have a primary interest in maintaining power over ourselves, over our lives, over our environments. Where I live in the United States, many people own firearms because they feel it is essential to have the power to defend themselves at all times. Accordingly, many of our popular movies and videos involve protagonists battling and destroying monsters, attackers, or political opponents. They can be seen as revenge fantasies, power fantasies, rejection or elimination fantasies. When I watch movies or TV shows with acute depictions of bullying, intimidation, or oppression, I feel compelled to fantasize about the aggressor being overpowered, even being punished. These instincts can reflect an inner need to feel that we are in power and in control. They can mean a rejection of our essential vulnerability to the forces of the world. Yet the Other is always at play in its many forms; and where there is Otherness, we must give up some measure of control to the situation.

This feeling of powerlessness - the notion that there are scenarios where we are subject to the powers of world, the unknown lurking in the darkness - is one of the most difficult things for people to process and familiarize themselves with. People make many, many life decisions just to escape this feeling of powerlessness. But the difficult and dark fact is that *we are powerless at times.* It is a hard fact. I have spent many days, weeks writing and processing these feelings that have emerged from within me. Many of them arose organically and pervasively following the birth of my daughter. This amazing, beautiful creature entered my world and reshaped my life, complicating my access to time and space, placing me in the hard machine of parental responsibility.

Powerlessness is a hard, dark, sticky sentiment. We often reject it and repress it into the pockets of our soul that live outside our awareness. We don't want to feel it or see it. It resides in *the shadow* - the Jungian concept that refers to the space in our psyche where we repress aspects of ourselves which we disallow or reject for various reasons. Jung also said that the shadow is "ninety percent pure gold" - meaning, it houses essential blocks of our humanness that we sequester from sunlight, from water, from warmth and visibility and affection. The shadow is a great Other, in some ways the greatest one, and as we uncover and unpack those areas of our shadow, we will find ourselves more deeply integrated and whole as valid multidimensional beings.

Relating to Others with Spirituality

We all have some space inside of us where we think about how we relate to the universe around us. We all have that intimate personal space. And this is typically the space we enliven and express in our spiritualities. We cultivate our relationship with our lives, the universe, a higher power, and ourselves. It becomes quickly challenging however when we want to share these parts of ourselves with others. These spaces diverge in each of us. We have differences in our outlooks, our language and definition, our belief systems. We each look at the world differently. We define our universes differently. We *feel* differently about these things.

I think we all crave to share our spiritualities with others. And unless we share the same tradition (and even then, to varying degrees), we see the world differently, and so this intimate part of ourselves becomes sequestered off from the rest of society. We are not able to share our intimate and spiritual selves with those around us, and this can create a sense of estrangement or frustration. We may truly enjoy our friends, our co-workers, our colleagues, our family; and yet this area becomes a sticking point. We aren't able to relate to others in this deeply personal area. Sometimes we try to build a bridge and share our ideas and viewpoints. But we are often met with difficult conversations that leave both parties feeling disappointed. People do not hear us. They do not want to hear us. They do not agree with us. They find our beliefs or ideas incorrect. They need to correct us or ignore us. They cannot abide the difference in our spiritualities. They cannot abide the fact that we are unique from them. They cannot tolerate this diversity of viewpoint.

But why is it this way? I think there are multiple factors at play here. I believe religion has, in many cases, been shaped and colored by political power or social engineering. That is, religion has become more than a purely personal spiritual pursuit. It has also become a domain of social conditioning, prescriptivism, dogmatism, coercion, and violence. Even if there is no overtly violent concept at play, spirituality has been charged with a desire to proselytize others, which is its own form of violence. To proselytize another is to interact with sincere desire for them to change their views of life. While this may not sound terrible on the surface, if we consider the sanctity and intimacy of the personal free will involved in choosing how we see the world, we see that the intention to change someone's mind is highly manipulative. It degrades the person and asks them to not be creative, but to merely follow. It asks them to degrade themselves by removing their volitional choosing.

It is important to note that this proselytizing attitude or any attempt to change someone else's viewpoint on things, or even refusal to accept that person's viewpoint, in fact registers in that person's energy. So while many of our classical and modern thinkers agree that the zone of conduct is in our outward, physical actions, we must understand that our intentions and energies also make an impression on the world around us. So, simply by desiring for others to change their viewpoint; or conversely, simply by not tolerating or accepting or being open to hearing someone else's point of view - exerts a kind of pressure on that individual. It fails to create a space for that person's individuality and unique personal context of reality to be received by you. By that same token, when we are truly open, truly willing to hear that other person's point of view, listen to their spirituality, make space to hear their beliefs - this can be remarkably new for that person. When they feel it, it may feel like something impossible has just happened. To actually express ourselves about this thing which is so strained and difficult and taboo - to finally get to express it and be accepted, encouraged, and nurtured, even by someone whose beliefs do not wholly align with ours - this is a remarkable experience. And how can we say this is not a path forward for the whole of our species? And this is something that is not merely done in the physical - by doing our personal development, working on ourselves so that we become more tolerant, we will change the qualities and behaviors of our energies, and that acceptance will be *felt*.

Being Ostracized

Many of us, in one way or another, know the pain of being different. We look back on our relationships from the past and we see how they have been changed by our own personal changes. We wanted to grow and evolve. We wanted to follow our purpose. But in so doing, we put ourselves at odds with the people in our lives. Our families, our friends, our colleagues. We felt stuck between worlds. Maybe we felt like we had to hide ourselves. And further still, we would find those individuals who would resonate with different facets of our personality. Some connected with us on personal history; some with political outlook; and others with our spiritual path. It is often those individuals with whom we had some spiritual affinity that we felt the closest kinship. But nevertheless, there was that feeling of segmentation.

I think that, as a society, we are simply too contracted in our ability to allow different cultures and viewpoints to enter our world. And through practices of Otherness, by bringing this idea into the forefront and making it a part of our personal viewpoint of ethics, we can create a world which is more tolerant in a deep, holistic sense. We can make a world where we listen to each other deeply and hear the viewpoints of one another. A world where we have some competencies in understanding the background of one another, of seeing the motivations behind our choices to color outside the lines. A world where we can finally feel understood - and practice our virtue of understanding others in a promising and remarkable development of Otherness.

Importance of Other People

Other people are truly essential to us. Sometimes I say this: we ourselves barely exist but for the lens of our relationships. We look at our values, our wants, and so many of them are bound up in other people. We want to do well so others will love us and think well of us. We serve to support our families or communities. We crave a status so that we will be validated in the eyes of others. To achieve greatness or fame means one is known by others. If we are not witnessed, we fear we never were.

Sometimes people interpret this concept through a secular lens. The idea is that we will eventually die off for good and truly vanish - but if we are remembered by others, we will live on indirectly through their memory. I feel this is a sad concept, because there are many great people who have been forgotten. I think of the women, the workers, the grandparents, the teachers who came and went and did not dent the register of the learned men who wrote the books. And it has been a great liberation for me to recognize, as expressed in the multidimensional lens, that life persists and our journeys will continue after this body decays. There is no shame in flying under the radar, and we can in fact live rich and authentic lives without the pressure to impress others.

What we truly want, I think, is to know that we are seen, felt, and experienced by others; and likewise, we want to see, feel and experience others. In a sense, we are living one eternal moment that moves and writhes and shimmies - and touching a single second of human connection is as great as anything. In this intimate co-creation, I think we commune with something fundamental in reality. My heart is your heart is every heart: we are softened for and by one another; the universe knows us and the mind feels a sense of completeness rendered in the eternal archetypes of humanity.

So, this is why I say that we ourselves barely exist, yet the others are like a redwood forest substantiating the fixtures of our life. And this is why, when a person enters my world, as a phone call or a bad driver or a barista or my family, I remind myself to say, "yes, I trust you. Yes, you are the right person to be here, now, in my life. In this moment, we are for each other. And I will do my part to be here fully for you and make space for our connection and its meaning here in this very moment." And all the while, meet them precisely where they are at, hearing the clarity of their personal, extemporaneous expression.

What amazes is me is how the power of an instantaneous connection with another person is available to us all the time. With just a look, a smile, an expression of care, we can share a moment of humanity with an absolute stranger.

Like some of us - perhaps not all - I have struggled at times to be a decent human being. I have in the past had a tendency to lash out at people in public when they got on my nerves. I sometimes feel embarrassed when I see videos online of someone having a meltdown in public, because I know that on an especially bad day, if I had a bit less energetic self-control, I might have wound up starring in such a video. And what has amazed me as I've worked on this trait is how spontaneous and easy is the choice to make someone new into your friend or your enemy.

So I ask myself: would you rather live in a world full of your friends - or a world full of your enemies? This is a choice within the scope of our creativity. People and relationships are immensely malleable. Even people we have a chequered history with can have the relationship reframed quickly if we present the particular qualities of presence and openness, affection and charity. If we show a person genuine kindness, if we evidence trust, they are likely to reciprocate, activating that natural bond of brotherhood which is latent between all human beings.

Being Shaped by Our Relationships

We can look at our relationships with others, as well, and see the way that we have been shaped by them. Our parents, our families, our friends, the people we knew. Can we accept them into the course of our Evolutionary Curriculum? Can we recognize their traits and accept them into our lives? Can we see those important people of our past and say, "yes, I accept you. I trust that you were the person for me in this life. Our relationship was a space of learning and growing. I extend myself into a space of *willingness* where our relationship took place. I am strong enough for this - and if I am not strong enough today, I trust that I will one day be strong enough to extend my *willingness* into the core of this relationship and recognize and validate it as interwoven with my Evolutionary Curriculum."

Growing Our Global Nervous System

When we practice otherness and apply ourselves to the challenges of the world around us, we are immediately confronted with all those different beliefs, lifestyles, values, and cultures at play in our world. It is a profound practice of otherness to extend ourselves to these strange flocks and come to understand them more deeply. And yet such an extension is a profound process of growing and expanding ourselves.

One principle which can be enormously helpful is to form meaningful personal relationships with people in the different regional and cultural pockets of our world. People from different states, different countries, different religions and ethnicities. Even those ones that we may have some fixed biased or negative impression about.

Get to know them. See their value. See their merit. It will make it permanently harder for you to casually dehumanize that group. Because you have entangled the nerves of your identity with this other person in this other group. And now, when you choose to condemn that group, you realize you are attacking your dear friend; and thereby attacking yourself, as well. You feel that pain because you have attacked someone you care about.

This is not a process of saying we agree or approve of everything in the world. Rather, this is about finding those individuals (and their individual qualities) that are admirable and meaningful to us. If we get to know someone, anyone, in an intimate level, we will begin to feel that vital dignity and life force within them. We will sense the humanity in the foundation of their souls. And we access a perspective wherein we no longer condemn them or coerce them or violate their will through a coercive thought about how they should change or be different or learn to think more like us. We will learn to treat them with humanity. Beyond this, we will doubtless be surprised at the level of intelligence and capability in these other groups.

Energetic Taste and Preference

One thing that I have noticed is that there is a kind of energetic 'taste' that people have. Certain preferences for particular feelings, ideas, schools of thought, tones. Just like an individual may listen to certain genres of music - baroque, grime, jungle, nü metal, acid jazz. Some of these appeal to us, and some of them don't. If we try them out for a while, we may - or may not - acquire a taste for them. This preference has a lot to do with our upbringing as well as our own individual characteristics.

Likewise with culture and energy, we can see that there is another kind of taste at play here. Individuals have energetic taste - and this will dictate the kind of norms, styles, philosophies, or intonations which are acceptable to them. Understanding this is a helpful step in moving past that divide and connecting with people who live in energetic characteristics that are different from ours. Knowing that there are different tastes of energy, how many of us can truly say that we can stand in a foreign energetic field and be at a harmony with it? This is a great undertaking and a tremendous opportunity for growth. If we lived in a world where people could do this, I think we would be living in a different world indeed.

The Other of Growth

Relating to the Other in a general sense is an important facet of our evolutionary curriculum. Why is this important? Because evolution means meaningful change in an outward direction. And if we do not extend ourselves, in some way, beyond the frontiers of our identity, beyond those familiar touchpoints that form the foundation for our psyche, then we will limit our growth a great deal. When we allow ourselves to cultivate a deeper relationship with the Other in many ways, this opens up pathways for a great deal of growth and learning.

One pertinent example of the Other would be a new understanding of ourselves. Given that our current self-concept is more or less how we identify with ourselves, a change to that self-concept is a kind of Other entering our reality. This change to our self-concept can come in the form of feedback, of outcomes, of ways we make people feel, of relationships. In many cases, when a person is confronted with some possibility of understanding themselves in a new way - especially if it makes them seem weak or immature - a person may find it too painful to confront it head-on. They may feel confronted by some new information that seems to challenge their identity. And so, they are unable to process the information. They apply some self-defense mechanisms to evade the information, its implications, and how it makes them feel. In this case, their ego would be protected, but the individual may not absorb much evolutionary value from the experience.

When we find ourselves facing challenging feedback, we can remember our personal ideas of nonviolence. We do not need to change. We are in touch with our essential dignity. And seeing the possibility of doing things better does not preclude our value as multidimensional people. Protected at our core by these positive personal truths, we may find that recognizing our own flaws and envisioning the possibilities beyond them need not be so painful. When I am stressed by the challenges of life, I try to remember that every challenge is new and fresh and alive for me. And I tell myself, "I am on the verge of a breakthrough. Something great is about to happen. If I can do this, I can do anything."

Truthfulness

Many areas of our society tolerate or even require untruths, deception, and distortion of reality. Competition, expediency, culture, and convention may seem to dictate that we are not truthful people in some cases. I think about the worlds of politics, of business, of finance, and even the complex dynamics of relationships and groups. Some people will even study and coach others on how to produce favorable reactions in others based on calculated, manipulated presentations of information.

While not everyone is enmeshed in a system of manipulated information, many of us have some area of our lives where there is an element of deception or inauthentic presentation to the world. From this standpoint, truthfulness itself looms like an Other. We may fear what truthfulness would do to us, because it could threaten the structures that we have built on top of misrepresentation.

A common case is people who make pervasive comments about themselves and others in order to project an artificially inflated view of themselves to impress others - a habit I call "perceptioneering". On a somewhat grander scale, I think about individuals in positions of power and influence who choose to continually distort information in order to protect their power structures.

For those who struggle with a gap of truthfulness, I offer some personal ideas to explore. For one, we are continuous and ongoing multidimensional people. Our fundamental being and validity is not enabled by any social function. We are already enough. And if we feel our life will truly begin when we move beyond some distortion, then this life is ours to have if we wish. Second, I offer some trust in the ongoing support and regeneration of the world. I tell myself: "If we choose to die by the truth, trust that life will rebear us anew into a better world." Or, more bluntly, "let the truth kill you."

As in all things, we can gather the sum of our insight, temperament, tact, and wisdom to authentically pursue a way forward. I am not encouraging indiscriminate radical honesty without regard for consequence. But where there is a will, there is an energetic way.

Anonymous Donations

There are days when I feel like the pipe fittings of my body have been loosed and I am hemorrhaging energy into the ether. I lie in bed and breathe heavy. I feel tender and vulnerable. It is hard to rouse myself to my feet or to any task.

I have come to understand these days as times of donation. In our house, we call this "pressure" or "bait". I would like to call it "hosting", with the idea that I am hosting nonphysical people in my field of energy. However, it is more likely that there is some process which is in need of my energy. So, I make it a point to allow others to connect to my energy who need it.

On these days, I need to give myself grace that I won't be as capable or productive. And I will understand that it is harder to accomplish things during this time. Sometimes I take some time off of work; and I sometimes have to eat some extra food with little discrimination. I just need to fuel and accommodate the process.

This may happen when something significant is going on - perhaps someone is ill or in hospice, or there is a major life transition happening. My energies, I hope and surmise, are being called into the chasms of these tectonic events. My hope is that they will soften landings and ferry my dear ones to their shores unharmed.

Multidimensional Pressure

There is one final Other I wish to discuss. It has cast a shadow over my life in many ways. It is in some ways quite mysterious. I hope to understand it better as I grow and develop in this life and beyond. For now, I will share my current understanding of it. This Other is called multidimensional pressure.

There are times in life where we will feel the energies in our field, in our environment, in our very world seem to close in on us, compress us, and drag us down. It may feel like friction, blowback, or diffuse discomfort. This is different from routine intoxication, because it persists despite a personal process of detox. Also, as someone who has worked with energy for a while, the quality of energies in multidimensional pressure is a bit distinct. It is a kind of diffuse heaviness that makes it challenging just to get through the day.

Multidimensional pressure tends to precede events, gatherings, or changes. In particular, I experience some amount of pressure in the days leading up to a class or workshop that we are organizing. It can be quite trying. On those days, I remember to not demand too much of myself, and to be understanding of my natural limitations based on the multidimensional process I am going through.

What precisely is the nature of multidimensional pressure? Sometimes, it seems to be a result of connecting energetically with a person or a process before it happens. It is almost like doing "energetic prep work" before an event, setting the stage energetically for the unfolding energetic field of the eventual gathering.

Other times, it can be a result of trying to undergo a personal change. Perhaps we are trying to make some personal adjustments to our behavior, our mindset, our beliefs about ourselves. This can come with some multidimensional pressure that almost seems to resist our personal changes. In this case, sometimes I theorize it is a force our ecosystem exerts on us, resisting the various changes that will occur when our energetic composition is altered. In this case, we sometimes talk about individuals going through a "bottleneck" - a period of more difficult constriction as we try to navigate ourselves through a personal change. In these cases, it is important to remain steadfast and equanimous in the face of challenges. Here is a place where a nonviolent posture can help a great deal. We keep our passions tempered, we stay clear-headed about those changes we are choosing for ourselves and our lives, and we proceed calmly through the storm.

One interesting and essential facet of multidimensional pressure is that it often does have a focal point or activity which can alleviate. This can be counter-intuitive, because we may feel like the appropriate response to pressure is simply to relax, stay centered, and weather the storm. However, there are cases where the pressure is due to a particular activity or objective that is ahead of us. Perhaps we planned to send an email, make a phone call, or organize something. It is like this is the 'lever' that the pressure has culminated around. Once we pull that lever, we may find that the pressure begins to subside shortly thereafter.

Following the experience of acute multidimensional pressure, I often find that there are amazing, effusive, wonderful fields of energy on the other side. For example, there may be difficult pressure before a class that ultimately has a magical, rich, satisfying quality to it. Yet I am still challenged by the acute difficulty of the preceding pressure itself. I do not fully understand yet why I have to undergo this difficult experience beforehand. I do think there are some opportunities to reframe how I understand the experience, to reshape my relationship with some new developments of maturity and even skill. But this is still a work-in-progress for me. And for me, the multidimensional pressure remains an imposing Other in my multidimensional journey.

7

EXPANSION

Let us not grow tired of discussions on the big ideas of life. For every time we speak of the infinite, it is a unique experience. We cast our momentary psychic contents into the darkness of sky and watch them work trails into the unknown. It is new every time we move ourselves in space.

WHEN WE CONNECT with the nonphysical side of reality, we experience an expanded mode of existence where customary boundaries and limitations may soften or vanish. As we experience expanded states and realities, we may be in touch with personal conditions that feel more advanced, more in tune with ourselves and the world.

Accordingly, these things are naturally connected with our evolutionary curriculum and our applications of otherness. These experiences are instructive, positive, edifying. They call us to become more mature and capable - when we swim in the expanse of nonphysical experience, we understand the importance of being responsible and stable, safeguarding essential structures that allow our lives to operate.

Ultimately, expanding beyond our ordinary boundaries helps us to expand and explore our humanness in its further reaches. Rather than taking us on an ego trip, I find these experiences are humbling and genuinely empowering. They can be an outlet from a more neurotic and frustrated experience within the physical. On some level, I think we require space as a basic human need; and the nourishment provided by the expansion of multidimensional experience can feel like high mountain water reaching the aching man who has missed moisture for many months.

I can remember periods of time where I craved acutely some kind of expansion or access beyond my ordinary life and its trappings. Shortly after graduating college, I was living on a couch in Brooklyn and had no career prospects or solid plans for myself. I watched Terrence McKenna videos where he inspired me to suck on salvia divinorum like chaw while lying on my back on the dark bathroom floor. I listened to Cocteau Twins and Harold Budd and Kate Bush with my ears up against the seam as though precious gas was leaking in from the great ocean. I remember the psilocybin afternoon with my roommate where the overcast clouds were October grey and the chilly air tasted like ancestral memories of Winter. I learned about out-of-body experiences and set myself on the carpet with my wolf blanket while Classon Avenue shone its amber glow on the ceiling. This was its own time, and its feeling still captivates me years later, even after everything I've done. The yearning stays with me.

Going Beyond the Body

There are many forms of expansion and outward exploration that are available to us as multidimensional individuals. One of the most stark and expressive forms of expansiveness occurs when we actually experience reality beyond the boundaries of the physical body. When we decouple ourselves from the physical body, it can feel like we are lifting out of an inert suit of armor. We become a being of nerves, thought, and energy. Our intentions become enacted immediately, transporting us to other areas of our house or neighborhood, or to various nonphysical contexts. We have clear, unambiguous insights which occur directly to our mind. We perceive clearly the content embedded in the fabric of energies.

While a comprehensive exploration of the out-of-body experience and its mechanisms are beyond the scope of this book, for those interested readers I can recommend the informative book *Demystifying the Out-of-Body Experience* by my colleague Luis Minero.

Decoupling from the Physical

While out-of-body experiences (or astral projection, as it is often called) provide a very immersed and comprehensive experience of reality beyond the body, it can be a challenging practice that is not intuitive or easy for everyone. To be honest, I would not characterize myself as naturally good at astral projection, and there have been limitations in my ability to effect experiences for myself over the years. However, something I have learned for myself which is too often overlooked by such practitioners is the value of all the experiences *preceding* the out-of-body experience. This means that simply *trying* to have an out-of-body experience can bring a wealth of new experiences which are therapeutic, edifying, and thrilling.

One of the great joys in life has been the simple, alarming joy of decoupling from the physical body. I lie on my back, relaxing, breathing deeply. I feel myself begin to slide out from the physical. There is a soft expansion in my head, my torso, my arms. It feels like *finally*. I am finally coming out of dense oak skin. I am finally coming out of the harsh tendrils of the world.

I am entering breathing space, a place of healing, a place where things are still stable, sensible, intelligent, and good.

For a long time, I would use this state as a signal that I'm getting closer to the out-of-body experience. I had been part of an organization that instructed on how to leave the body and all the ways that we can validate, explore, and develop our understanding of a deeper, subtler reality which is more fundamental than the physical. And so, rather than enjoying the value of this experience outright, I would feel myself starting to leave the body but be held back. I might start focusing on my breath, which vanishes when you are out of the body. I might start to feel a weird itching or a tickling in my throat. Or a painful knot in my back. Or I would just never quite get out of my head. I rarely had the experience I had set out to have.

But, by learning to value the decoupled state, that very chill and delicious expanded state where I'm decoupled from the physical body, I've found a new angle to value the experience. And this decoupled state, to me, is a much better value proposition to the majority of people. I don't think it's hard to achieve, and there are a ton of skills to learn in how we can effect and have control in that state.

So, what happens in these experiences? I begin to feel more expansive. I feel more open. I can feel and perceive and work with energies more clearly. Sometimes it's a funny feeling. I feel silly and huge. There is something hilarious about the feeling sometimes. Sometimes I can perceive nonphysicals very clearly, at times. I will hear them speaking or saying things to me. It is typically warm, kind, positive things. A couple of times I have heard these kind caretakers say things alarmingly kind to me.

Inevitably, I wake up in the morning feeling more clear, more refreshed than I would have otherwise. So I preach the therapeutic practice of decoupling from the body, even if we are not able to achieve a full out-of-body experience.

No Belief Survives a True Experience

I sometimes say: no belief truly survives an encounter with nonphysical reality. This does not mean that every idea we have vanishes - but it clarifies to us the meagerness of our attempts to subdue our world into a crude submission by the presumed dominance of our thoughts.

When we are in an expanded state, interacting with the reaches of ourselves in this nonphysical state, sensing more comprehensively the completeness of our multidimensional reality, we will drink an experience which offers an almost continuous source of learning and new awareness. When we work with energy, when we decouple from the physical body, when we find ourselves more aware while outside the body at night, we experience the oceanic reality in greater magnitudes. Our ideas feel smaller, less encompassing. Of course - how could they not? We are so accustomed to harboring our ideas and harboring our vision of reality. We hold close our worldview. In some ways, through our worldview, we claim to own the world. To control it. And perhaps that is a key point of why we are so territorial of our worldviews, how strongly we can react when they are challenged. Our worldviews give us a sense of control over our world. But when we are having a truly multidimensional experience, we relinquish that control. We enter the ocean. Rather than harboring our universe encased in a snowglobe, we immerse ourselves in the vast, rushing aliveness of universal experiences. Immediately, the meagerness, the smallness, the pittance of our ideas is felt immediately like a calcium tablet dissolving in the rushing liquid space.

We realize that our ideas are, at best, handholds in that vast space. We cannot control or contain the dazzling fields of reality. Why would we want to? It must come from fear. But when we feel that space, we feel that we are indeed provided for. And more than an enhancement of our ideas, we experience a change in temperament. The multidimensional experience teaches us. It shows us a bit of what life is and how we are in relationship with it. It tempers us by showing us a way to let go of control and partner with the energy of things. Like one in the ocean, we learn to graduate from clinging to ideas to instead swimming in a sea of meaning and experience. This is why we say that our beliefs never truly survive an authentic experience of the nonphysical reality.

Expanding to Creativity

By developing a relationship with contexts of reality which are not limited to this physical dimension, we are able to expand our imagination and experiences into truly novel territory for ourselves. Where does our imagination come from? So much of it comes from how we sense and perceive and tune in to different frequencies of energies. We are not merely rolling dice in the fires of our nervous system - we are exploring new concepts in the energies of imagined realities. Moreover, these imagined realities may have some basis in the nonphysical world. Perhaps they are already coalescences within that global collective psyche.

By developing our relationship with exploring energies, feeling new energies, developing the suppleness and sensitivity and openness of our own energies, we open ourselves up to considering new possibilities and avenues for exploration.

Beyond this, however, our ability to actually explore the nonphysical world is tremendously powerful, allowing us to get a sense of the different personalities, communities, philosophies, and qualities of living that exist through the vast expanse of possibility.

Exploring the Nonphysical World

Let us talk more about new experiences and insights that happen when we go outside the body.

When we are in the lucid dream-state, we are often inter-acting with people who are new to us. They have new names and personalities. We are experiencing new facets of life. New cultures. And these are experiences similar to our experiences in the physical body but also quite acute and intimate and special for us. We get to know new people and meet them and experience their energies.

And because these people are often those who already exist on the other side - that is, they are not currently undergoing a lifetime - it is an important and groundbreaking development of our expansion, universalism, otherness, maturity - to develop relationships with people who are currently in the nonphysical. So we, living in this complex web of relationships, can develop our relationships in and out of the body. And our ontology, our placement of being, begins to straddle that multidimensional boundary. And we become more expressly multidimensional beings. We will feel we are half in this world but also a part of us inhabits this other nonphysical world.

This duality, multidimensionality, is a truly healthy devel-opment for an individual. We start to see this physical world more easily for what it is: a place for expression, learning, and experimentation. "All the world is a stage" - and this is physical world is an important space for all kinds of creations. We see how this world is a staging place; and we also see how much essential reality exists in that nonphysical world. That world of the collective psyche. We form bonds with people in the nonphysical, and they are like anchor points. So we, as network-people, as lattice-selves, are able to operate in a way which appreciates both sides of the coin. We are able to operate in this physical world in a way which reflects a greater understanding, since we are more tuned into in the nonphysical.

If we have no knowledge of the nonphysical world - if we are divorced from that active collective psyche space - we will miss so much of the picture. But when we learn to work with some feet in the nonphysical world, we can cater *a more complete vision* which incorporates a view of both of these worlds.

This other world is already a part of our lives. It plays out through the energy fields of our world, affecting the way that we think and feel. It is there underneath, like background music and temperature and humidity. Just as there is work to be done in this physical world, there is a wealth of neglected spaces and communities in the nonphysical. The nonphysical world and its influences function like a hidden diet of thought-forms which become incorporated into the body of society. How can we claim to move forward lucidly if we are not aware of this second, hidden world? How can we claim to help the world if we have no clue about this second world and how to co-create across the boundary line? Especially when we can effect change in this nonphysical world for zero dollars and only the energy of our intentions and manifestations?

Mature People in the Nonphysical

By developing our relationship with our nonphysical helpers or spirit guides, we can begin to see how there exists more evolved and developed wisdom and functioning than we see generally throughout this physical world. These nonphysical individuals, due to their condition, are able to operate in a way that is quite distinct from us - we simply will not acquire and process information the same way that they will.

We can further explore this nonphysical aspect of life as a kind of anthropological lens. What are humans doing outside of the physical dimension? What does human society look like beyond the physical? These are legitimate questions. There is a tremendous wealth of experiences to be had and insights to be explored.

What does a highly evolved society look like in the nonphysical? We may see that many of the rules or norms that we consider standard do not apply in these places. For example, our societies are often based on the idea that people need some existential threat in place to force them to work. People must work for their own food, shelter, medicine. In a more evolved society, we will likely see people balancing personal freedoms with collective cooperation. If everyone operated in a silo, there would be no collective results utilizing everyone's strengths; but if everyone was told what to do by some outside authority, there would be no sense of personal responsibility in place to motivate the individuals to align their work with their authentic evolutionary challenges and interests. We come to see that the ways we work in our society, and we say, "this is human nature and it does not change" - this is not the way things must always be. But this is accomplished by servicing the root, by helping people grow, by healing, growing, and educating society from the first. Not by policing behavior and coercing people to defy the natures that they have co-created with their local cultures and bodies.

Timeless Identity

One of the greatest changes to one's sense of expansion comes when we recognize that we live more than once. This lifetime is a mere expression of our potential and our creativity, our education and learning, our journey onward. We are on a multi-millennial voyage through these lives.

When I was younger, I would think of my life as a relatively short line with two endpoints - two black dots connected by a line. There was a sense of madness about the whole thing. I could not stomach my life being a single black line on a page which terminates into untold silence. So I felt a tremendous pressure to transcend that line. We must make ourselves to be more than this! How can we do so? Should we live for a cause; die for one? Should we be loud and change things? Every passing year, I would compare myself to others, thinking about what they accomplished by the time they were as old as I was.

And yet, there are those who achieve renown and success, and they may not feel fulfilled with that outcome. It rings much hollower than they would have expected before they accomplished things. Because true satisfaction would only come from something deeply personal, not a mere outward event.

This whole situation changed when I exploded that little black line. I let the line ride. Off the page, off the table, out the window. Yes, there is ample space for us and our lives. We have time to be weird and funky. We have time to tend to those tiny, immeasurable things that we truly care about. We have time to sit and be quiet and listen to others. To sit and listen to nothing, too. It is not strictly necessary to discard this "one-life" idea in order to find this sense of peace. But it helps, a great deal. It helps things make more sense.

While I don't hear this said very often, I think that the many-lives concept is very logical and intuitive. I am happening now - I was born and I will die. So, I presume this will happen again. Once more, I will be born, and I will die. And again, and again. Why isn't this simple premise identified more often?

But it is more than a hypothesis. When we touch the space between lives - when we develop a more intimate familiarity with the nonphysical world, which I sometimes call the world of psyche and energy. It is analogous to the collective unconscious of Jung in some respects; but it is more refined and developed in articulation. Less murky, phenomenological, mysterious. It is not an unconscious, but a vibrant living space populated by a vast spectrum of communities, cultures, and people. A place for exploration, experience, and learning. Perhaps, a more fundamental plane than this physical world we inhabit.

So, when we perceive and experience the nonphysical world, we touch the space between lives and come to understand our nature on a deeper level. We see that we exist in a continuum. This life is a single event. Beyond it, we will endure, as we have endured, for a series of lifetimes. And we come to know ourselves as eternal beings, enduring beings. As beings who dwell beyond space, immaculate and immeasurable, in an expanse of creative opportunity. We exist in the brilliant breathing canvas. Through our experiences, this becomes a part of who we are, how we understand ourselves.

As a result of these experiences, we may find that our priorities can change. Our limited perspective of only existing for a single lifetime created a needless urgency throughout life. But, now knowing that we will exist for the long haul, this urgency dies down a bit. We are able to focus on all the things we truly value. And come to refine our understanding of what is important.

What is important, after all? Perhaps it is our intimate ideas, our relationships, our creations and co-creations. It is our evolutionary curriculum - our pursuit of intimate coursework and learning, evolving and educating ourselves and others. And we come to know better who we are. What motivates us, what is important for us. We refine the ideas around our identity. We become, as it is true for me, a more advanced version of ourselves. We enter into this next stage, clothed with ideas and tools and experiences which suit us far better than those we had donned previously.

Ecstasy of Balance

I am astonished how I live with energetic blocks and deficiencies. I am an incomplete person, and I most always forget this. What happens is, in certain instances I am relaxing or working energies, and I feel a certain block or emptiness of my energy body start to relax. I feel the energies flowing through this area. And I feel how much this blockage was tied to me feeling insecure, anxious, unhappy. Persistent throughout life. It amazes me the embedded unhappiness in our energies.

Energies flow into this space and it is like a keystone slotting in. I feel a kind of completeness, a relaxation. A key that turns and releases the tension. And it amazes me that life can feel okay - when those energetic disturbance gets resolved for some time.

This is an expansive experience because we don't realize that we can feel whole, complete, at peace. We are always, our energies are always, works in progress. And there are always additional layers of wellness, states which are freer of disturbance. Even if we had the world's most talented energy therapist work on us for one year, we would still have energetic issues to work on. This is because our energies are a reflection of our behaviors - our thoughts, feelings, emotions, attitudes. As long as we are human, we will be imperfect, learning beings. And this imperfection will show up in the form of energetic disturbances or issues in our energy body.

We are like travelers coming in from the cold - the feeling of an energetic resolution will always be exquisite.

Putting Top-Shelf Ideas on Hold

Big Ideas rush to the doorway like solicitors. When we talk about spirituality, we bubble up ideas about God, Source, Spirit, the beginning of all things. People want to understand the fundamental and absolute concepts. I call these topics 'distant metaphysics', because they deal with absolute, final, endpoint concepts.

One of the reasons people want to know about these things is because they are a major component of some spiritual traditions. In the past, these absolute ideas have been used for political leverage - someone tells other people to join their religion or else God will punish them. Some people feel comfortable casually attributing transient human qualities to the essential foundation of reality. I imagine someone putting Groucho Marx glasses on a giant white star. We take our frustrations and blow them up - "I am mad, but the universe is furious!"

People want to know about God because this concept has been swung around people's heads since they were children. They want to know how a mature multidimensional view fits with a traditional religious one.

Like all personal ideas, each person's interpretation and understanding is personal to them. In terms of designating a God or absolute concepts for reality, I really think this is personal, and has so much to do with what feels right for a person's unique emotional, philosophical, cultural makeup. I recognize the importance of feeling like you have a personal relationship with a divine protector. I also recognize the importance of local spiritual communities. So, I think it is up to each one of us to have our own definition - our own unique and personal set of language, ideas, relationships - that connect us with life at large.

These absolute concepts are, indeed, personal, and I want to ensure a space where you feel comfortable and affirmed in protecting and developing your personal relationship with reality, however you define things.

On an impersonal level, I think there is a somewhat more mature point of view on things where we could hopefully find connection. As we explore multidimensional experiences, we will be able to participate in many experiences of tremendous expansion, extended cognition, greater awareness, expansion of self, and more. These experiences are indeed expansive, and they show us the limitations of how we saw things previously - how narrow was our viewpoint. This dynamic - realizing that our understanding is limited in most cases, and even in our more expanded modes of experience we recognize the humongous space that exists *beyond* our comprehension - is an experience common to us all. Like so many of the conclusions of Socrates in his dialogues, we see how much more there is to know in the universe. And one of the most common remarks of those who have truly revolutionary, earth-shaking expansions of consciousness is that these experiences could not be boiled down to words. The experiences were alarmingly vast, consequential, laden with meaning. And there was no way to put it back into the constricted, one-dimensional pipefittings of our language.

So, the conclusion here is that top-shelf ideas, those concepts which are truly humongous and reside in the foundations and edgepoints of existence, are simply beyond the capacity of our language. And while we can have greatly expanded experiences, those experiences are glimpses of the titanic space that immerses us in all directions - even in our expansions, there is so much more to know. For this reason, I don't pay huge heed to the biggest of ideas.

Far better that we learn to swim than to make claims over the ocean. Let us balance ourselves and live wonderful lives.

Operating Through Energy

Language is spellcraft. Words articulate energy. The words themselves do not define the reader's experience. It is the energy of the writer, embedded in the threads of lettering, that we experience when we read.

This is why I take language so seriously. I emphasize the creation of personal ideas, rendered in your personal language, so that you will feel comfortable expressing your native, nascent personal energies into the words that are actual for you. This is why I urge against the use of indoctrination through fixed ideas and forced definitions.

And as we learn to work more with energy, to operate through energy, to become more self-aware of the energy we are already using and experiencing in our lives - we will begin to move into and out of language more easily. We will see the energy itself, that tissue-fabric underneath and animating the language. The wizard puppeteer behind the tiny wooden dolls marching onstage.

And we will see those ways that we can operate freely without language, by using our awareness, our forces, our subtle perceptions to maneuver and articulate energies themselves. This gives us a doorway to become more adept on the energetic level. To become less literal with words. To see the words as tools, faithful servants, great heroes in their right, but also to see the work undertaken in the arrangements of energies. We see the words as tools, but we see the energies as the true craft of creation.

8

GOOD

E*very person around you is essential to your life purpose. They are woven into you like the threads of your skin.*

WE COME to ask ourselves how we should live? What is the protocol for life, given all that we have discussed? Of course, it is entirely your journey. You will define it and create it and co-create it with all those beautiful beings who inhabit this charmed life you are undertaking. At the same time, we can develop several ideas to help us to understand what a worthwhile life looks like.

And moreover, what does it mean to do good in this world? Things are complicated, and the hope is that a more refined understanding through this multidimensional lens will allow us to simplify or clarify or amplify some choices in how we can use our time and our energies wisely.

We Deserve Challenges

In a lot of ways, we look at the problems of the world and we are disappointed. We feel they should be fixed. We are frustrated. Remember however the things that we said in the Curriculum chapter. "This is your moment. This is your life. It belongs to you. It is yours and it is of you and for you." So these things we experience in life, the problems and all, are not simply impediments. "The obstacle is the way," as Marcus Aurelius said.

So, when taken at a global and more collective level, we see that the problems of the world are the collective challenges we all face as a reflection of our evolutionary curriculum. Like the blind men exploring the elephant, we each chart our own course through the challenges of our contemporary world. But make no mistake that the challenges of our world are, to some degree, intentional, and they are personal to us. They are reflections of that collective psyche, and therefore they are emanating from our own psyches, to some degree. They are a part of our shared multidimensional reality together on this planet.

And so it is our project. It is a part of our garden. Let us tend to the garden. Let us endeavor to nurture our plants and remind them how beautiful they are. And when they come into bloom and we shed a tear we will pretend that we are not surprised that they turned out quite so beautiful as they did.

Beyond Morality

I have always had a problem with morality. When I was fifteen, I spoke at a school assembly about moral absolutes, and I argued that moral absolutes did not exist. However, I didn't prepare well, and spoke poorly. Many people in my class - whom I loved and admired - came away from that assembly vexed with me: why would I be so callous to say that horrible acts of degradation are not morally bad in an absolute sense? I still think of this assembly today; perhaps once per week.

I still struggle to articulate my concerns about moralistic thinking; it is a complex topic that hits me deeply. But my concerns remain. I will do my best to articulate them here, as it pertains to our multidimensional lens.

First, I do endorse conventional notions of right and wrong as a social shorthand for acceptable conduct. But when we define our moralities as absolute, or wield them as fundaments of reality, this changes our viewpoint: it takes our definitions of how the world *should* be and makes them the building blocks of our world. It allows us to define our world and its challenges, not in terms of curiosity, but of blame. The world's troubles are caused by 'bad' or 'evil' behavior.

And by focusing on bad people, this mindset tends to shift attention away from understanding our challenges. We may miss, for example, the troubling reality that aggressors were themselves victims; which does not excuse their behavior but complicates it in a human sense. We may miss new ways to intervene in psychological, social, or systemic challenges as a co-creator of a better future. More than ever, I see that this world needs a reformation of our energetic ecology in favor of healthy, balanced energy; this energy is not achieved by casting aspersions on others, but by tending to the whole world as one's garden.

Focusing on bad people also primes us to think about punishing the wicked over nurturing and caring for those who were wronged. It permits a mindset of cruelty, which is often driven by unconscious desires for power, for simplicity, for easy satisfaction in the face of a complicated world.

It may be easier to say that the world's problems are evil than to say that they are human. Because, by saying they are human, we are forced to sit with them and see how we might have that capacity in us, as well. That we could be condemned by our fellows one day. And to see, critically, that there are those moments of difficulty where - for now - we may not have the power to transmute darkness into light. To sit with our own powerlessness is acute and difficult; it alone changes us.

Recall Chapter 6: we said that powerlessness is one of the most impactful facets of our personal shadow, something that we struggle to process. Morality may allow us to reject our feelings of powerlessness by defining a cosmic ruleset that gives the last word of life to a blazing accusation.

When we had this assembly at school, one of my favorite teachers spoke at the end and said, "I continue to believe in moral absolutes, because I believe that anything which degrades or assaults the dignity of a human being is wrong." I deeply agree with his sentiment. My only note is to blur the boundary lines: let us look beyond the act, into the human; beyond the ruleset, into space; and unpack the possibilities embedded in our relationships with every other person, whether we choose to see them or not.

Outcomes of Our Energy

Our choices are not as simple as they seem. In a single moment, we feel that we can make any choice and it has no reality except as a simple movement of the body, selection of the mind, tiny ripple of physical behavior. But in truth our choices exist in the panoramic space of multidimensionality. Our actions are more than physical - they are expressions of energy and psyche. They reverberate into this hidden world where they co-create the situations of our lives and the lives of others.

This may sound quite abstract and esoteric, but we can actually *feel* the outcomes of our actions in the form of energy. When we make a choice, there is that reverberation, like the banging of a gong. And like an intelligent tuning fork, we can learn to identify and understand the tone, intonation, and response of our actions. Like a xylophone player, we learn to strike the musical bars and create new frequencies, composites, expressions, feelings, atmospheres and ambience.

Multidimensional Ethics

As we gain experience in life, we all develop a certain awareness of how our actions reverberate. We sense the quality of our intentions and receive subtle feedback from our outside world. This awareness may accompany an explicit energetic practice or simply reflect a heightened intuition of when and how things work better for ourselves and others.

As this awareness matures, it coalesces and becomes an essential organ of how we operate: a refined sense of our more *optimal* behavior in life. This refined sense allows us to develop a healthier and more co-creative relationship with our world.

This personal attribute of optimal behavior we sometimes call our "multidimensional ethics". Like conventional ethics, it is based on a thoughtful, dispassionate sense of which choices will yield the best outcomes. Unlike conventional ethics, it is rooted in awareness of our shared multidimensionality, which may follow a different set of protocols. Notably, it eliminates certain hard boundaries and recognizes that thoughts and intentions carry an energetic charge and have the capacity to affect the outside world.

For example, we may recognize that we indulge in certain forms of dishonesty, and that this dishonesty is actually cultivating a less genuine personal state of mind. This less genuine mindset, in turn, may affect the quality of our energies and place us in greater resonance with other people - nonphysical people - who have a similar quality of being dishonest or ingenuine. Having such a quality of nonphysical company would predispose us to greater rates of intoxication, which may make us feel less and less like *ourselves*. And so, in relationship with our personal multidimensional ethics, we may decide that this particular form of dishonesty is counterproductive for us. By changing the thoughts that initiate this behavior, and changing that behavior in our lives, we cut off all of those downstream countereffects which were compromising our life in several ways.

Multidimensional ethics are personal. They are something we each develop inwardly, according to ourselves. We can define them in whatever way we like. They can exist in the form of a personal code that we write down somewhere. Or it can exist on a more subtle level. It certainly will exist on a subtle level, to some degree, because any level of multidimensional ethics will have some discernment around energetic quality and some resolve around how to interface with particular frequencies of energy. But it can also exist in the form of specific decisions to do or not do certain things. In our multidimensional ethics, we may have some ideas which are more present for us at the moment, which are more pertinent to our evolutionary moment. And as those behaviors or changes become more ingrained and digested into our behavior, we will likely find new things to focus on over time.

One of the most interesting and cross-disciplinary applications of multidimensional ethics I have used in my life is the use of key affirmative phrases in order to re-tune my energies. Recently, I wrote down the phrase, "prioritize health", which helped me to take greater awareness of my holistic multidimensional state and attend to it throughout the day. Previously, I tended to allow my multidimensional state to suffer throughout the day, to fall a bit into disrepair or energetic entropy. I would periodically recite the phrase inwardly and *dial in* to the frequency of the idea, reinforcing an energetic reprogramming that began when I started my relationship with the phrase.

I used this phrase "prioritize health" for several days. It kept me more self-aware, less single-mindedly focused on those tasks in front of me. I cultivated a greater state of presence. Over time, the phrase fell out of use, but the energetic reprogramming remained in its way, suspended in the cellular fluid of my multidimensional self.

Enmeshed Worlds

In previous chapters, we noted the importance of being aware of both worlds we live in: the physical world and the nonphysical one. These worlds influence one another - these are interconnected and interenmeshed. If we do not learn to address and work with our nonphysical world, we may be like a beautifully rendered puppet, fully decked out with clothes and skills, and no control over our strings. The nonphysical world affects our feelings, thoughts, motivations. And conversely, becoming a mature co-creator means understanding the nonphysical world so we can facilitate more advanced and functional realities for ourselves and others.

The word 'functional' is key. It is not that the world is wrong or bad or sinful or unholy - it simply doesn't work as well as I feel it could. And that possibility of greater functionality extends into deeply humane realms of experience. By understanding multidimensional ethics, we see that what we consider 'good' behavior may be just functional behavior. It is behavior that works in some alignment with a healthy evolutionary pattern for developing our lives and a collective world for everyone.

What does this functional behavior look like? It has many different looks and shapes, and each person will cultivate their own functionality as an expression of their multidimensional ethics. However, there are some core patterns and dynamics which I believe are common to developing, maturing, advancing, and healing this world. One of the most central is the healthy exchange of energies in support of healthier energetic ecologies in our world.

Assistance

In general, we help others through the exchange of energy. We are energy-composite beings. By exchanging healthy energies with others, we enrich them and afford them opportunities to pursue new perspectives on life, on themselves, and on how their choices and behaviors impact the world around them.

We often call this "assistance" - that is, the healthy and humanitarian donation of energies to others. This is one of the reasons I strive to respect and honor all spiritual traditions. A prayer circle of any particular denomination could potentially be doing a great deal of assistance.

More recently, I have begun organizing healing circles. I meet with friends or our community through our non-profit and work with energy, donating our energies for the betterment of others. These healing circles may focus on people or affairs anchored in the physical dimension; but the energies often go beyond, addressing factors at play in the nonphysical.

In our nonphysical world, which is like our collective psyche, there are many people and many communities in a variety of states. Many of them are imbalanced, perhaps in an aggravated entropic state. For these communities, donating our healthy and balanced energies can truly transform them and support their healing from the inside-out. Our energies can help to reform the relationships, the culture, the atmosphere of these communities. Providing these individuals and patterns with a healthy dose of energy allows the possibility of recovery to begin. It may give individuals a heightened self-awareness, sensory relief, functional stability. This type of work is most always done in concert with nonphysical evolutionary guides, also known as spirit guides or helpers.

By helping to heal and stabilize individuals and communities throughout the nonphysical world, we often address the *underlying cause* to so many of the ills of society. This can be a remarkable change from the typical pattern: we look at the world and see many challenging situations; we want to make a difference by intervening in physical affairs; but the physical intervention feels insurmountable or our efforts fall short. When we just look at physical manifestations, we may overlook the *underlying energetic ecologies* which are driving the attitudes, feelings, and behavior patterns which precipitate broader social and global outcomes.

Of course, there are many factors that make the world work as it does. There are cultural factors - people need to feel heard, they need to be recognized with dignity, and they need to co-create their new reality in partnership with others and with their life experiences. Deeper still, we can say that the *root cause* of many of our issues is our immaturity as individuals and collectives.

But our situations are deeply exacerbated by imbalanced multidimensional realities. In many cases, unhealthy nonphysical ecologies can exert great pressure and momentum to maintain certain patterns of behavior, thought, and energy. As long as we have entrenched nonphysical communities imposing, for example, dogmatic, indoctrinating, and supremacist attitudes, there will be pressure to conform in the physical world. Because the pressure is energetic in nature, it can be fascinating to see how various social groups take on similar frequencies over time; different political groups, ethnic groups, or religious groups, for example, could each manifest a supremacist ideology with a *similar energetic character* - even if each group is *opposed to the other.*

So, one way to develop the maturity and awareness of our

global society - in a way that is unified, across both worlds - is to partner with our evolutionary guides in our practice of energetic assistance. This assistance provides a 'way up' for those populations who are stuck in stagnant dimensions and may be ready to move on to a more functional way of living. In working with our guides in this way, we will find our own conduct and lucidity will naturally improve as a result of connecting more deeply with their rarefied energies. And so, working beyond the physical world, we find avenues for transformation that can make a tremendous difference while integrating meaningfully with our personal, spiritual lives.

Your Guides are Here

To that extent, make no mistake - you will be partnering with your evolutionary guides on this. They are most likely here with you, at this moment, as you read this. Perhaps take a moment. Take a breath. If you want, you can close your eyes for a moment - and recognize that presence in your space. Recognize they are with you. Can you feel it? Sense it, taste it, touch it? The energies are there. They are palpable. This person, these people - they are here for you. With care and kindness and love, for they care for you so deeply in this regard. They have been with you many times along the way. They have woven themselves into your life like fabric - like a red thread, luminous and caring, a red thread of victory to assist you in binding your experiences together into this tapestry of co-creation. Yes, of course - it is a co-creation, for they could not do it without you - without your choices, your actions, your dedication.

So, consider taking a moment and being aware of your evolutionary guides as they have been present to support you and help you identify the things which will be beneficial to you in your evolutionary journey through life.

Your evolutionary guides will be present whenever it is most appropriate for them to be. And they will be there for you when you need them most. They tend to appear when we are engaging in some material or activity which is essential to our evolutionary purpose. They come when there is meaning, value, and impact to their presence. Their contribution is usually through that energetic presence. With your evolutionary guide, you co-create new fields of energy which are more astutely attuned to the evolutionary opportunities of the moment. And so, working with them, you are able to make something far greater than you could have done on your own. Let us take a moment to appreciate this co-creation - the fact that something truly great, truly intimate and personal, was in fact made in partnership with those ones who are loyal and love you and support you in this intimately multidimensional space.

FROM ALL THOSE **evolutionary helpers on the other side, I wish to thank you and congratulate you for taking the time to read these ideas and explore these concepts.** It is not that these ideas are perfect or ideal or even totally appropriate for you. But they are an opportunity, a big space, a new canvas for you to reconsider your own life and your own beliefs. What do you believe? What is important for you? How will you charge your life with meaning and impact? Will you change yourself in addition to the world? How will you make your love a thing of power and leverage your bonds with others to mobilize a change? It is all up to you.

I wish you the absolute best and I am thrilled to participate as your fellow, as your friend, as your co-creator - in this life and beyond.